Reseach: Robin Prijs, Esther Prijs
Language corrections: Jane Upchurch McNeill
Editing: Esther Prijs
Graphic Design: Robin Prijs
Publisher: JMI Foundation, LoveUnlimited Ministries

The Bible translation that is used in this book is the NKJV, unless it says differently.

Contact details:
LoveUnlimited Ministries / JMI Foundation
Van Oldenbarneveltplein 104
3317ET DORDRECHT
The Netherlands

Phone: +31 85 104 5555
E-mail: info@love-unlimited.org

Website:
www.love-unlimited.org

The Anointed

BRIDE

Robin Prijs

Special thanks…

To God, for challenging me to study this topic and for granting me the knowledge, wisdom and understanding I needed. This has been quite a journey, which I value a lot!

To Abba Anointing Oil, for allowing me to use their insights and study on the meaning of the fragrances.

To my wife, Esther, for always being there for me, for being such a great and blessed help and for always supporting me in everything I do.

To a brother, who rather has his name not mentioned. For teaching me a lot about the Anointing and the use of Anointing Oil in several occasions. For drawing my attention to this subject and the meaning of it. Much of what I know I owe to his teachings and to what he showed me through his actions in faith.

CONTENTS

"God's Anointing is something I cannot live without in my ministry or Kingdom life in general. Robin Prijs has done a thorough job using his gift of teaching to bring clarity to this intriguing subject. His exhaustive research will help you get a better understanding of this all important element of power. I plan to use this writing as a handbook for years to come!"

Terry MacAlmon
International Worship Leader

INTRODUCTION

In the ancient times, the Anointing Oil was always given a very important and prominent place among the people and nation of Israel, and among the Christians in the New Testament. But somehow the use and meaning of Anointing Oil has lost its meaning to the contemporary Church. It has never lost its meaning in general, but to us, as the Church of today, it no longer means what it used to mean to the people of Israel and to the first Christians. What has changed? God? Or the Church? We know that God never changes, so it must be us. With this book and study it is my aim to give the knowledge, insight and understanding, about the Anointing and the Anointing Oil, back to the Church.

I have read many studies about Anointing Oil, and much of the same teachings can be found in this study as well, but much of the insights I have found are rarely mentioned in studies or not mentioned at all. On the one hand, this is quite exciting. But on the other hand it makes you wonder how much insight we – as the Church – have lost over the course of the last centuries. But that loss can end here and now.

As you read this study, I want to encourage you not to use these insights, knowledge and wisdom as your final answer or to merely accept it as a new doctrine. It is my hope, desire and prayer that you rather use this study as your starting point, as a handle and a tool, to find the incredible rich truth behind it and to find what God wants to say to you personally. Information is just information, just a bunch of knowledge, when God doesn't open our eyes. The very first mistake mankind made was to start trusting on knowledge, which showed a desire to be independent of God and which is a fruit of pride. Only the Spirit of God can make the Word of God alive in you, as if you can read the Word in different dimensions. That gift of wisdom and understanding is not meant for a select group of people, but is available to all those who choose to depend on God, who take the time to study His Word and who set their heart to find the answers, with the attitude to not give up until they've found what they were looking for. That is what Jesus meant in Matthew and that is what I encourage you to do as well.

Ask, and it will be given to you; seek, and you will find; knock, and it will be opened to you. For everyone who asks receives, and he who seeks finds, and to him who knocks it will be opened.
Matthew 7:7-8

I would like to add something more to that. Not only is it important to ask, search and knock, it is just as important to test everything. In times like these, where there are so many opinions and different types of beliefs, even within the Church, the only real handhold and rock you have is the Word of God. Everything that comes from the Spirit of God is never in contrary to the Word of God.

Do not quench the Spirit. Do not despise prophecies. Test all things; hold fast what is good. Abstain from every form of evil.
1 Thessalonians 5:19-22

As you read this study, I want to encourage you to open your Bible and to look up all the Bible verses as well. Ask the Holy Spirit to grant you the gift of wisdom, insight and understanding. When the words you speak to God are matching the desire of your heart, and when they are in line with the Word of God, it shall be granted to you.

The Anointing, the Anointing Oil and everything that is associated with it, are appearing quite often in the Bible. But did you know that there are 345 Bible verses in 201 chapters, that are talking about it? And did you know that the name 'Messiah' or 'Christ' means 'Anointed One' and that that name appears 596 times in the Bible? Is God trying to say something to us? I believe so.

Robin Prijs

Worship God! For the testimony of Jesus is the spirit of prophecy.
Revelation 19:10

CHAPTER 1

THE ORIGIN OF ANOINTING

When we start reading the Bible, in our search for the meaning of Anointing and Anointing Oil, then we can find the first use in the book of Genesis, where Jacob Anointed Bethel. But when you are a frequent reader of the Word, then you know that not everything in the Bible is in chronological order. When we take all the parts of the Bible that speak about this topic, and place them in chronological order, then we can establish some sort of timeline. I say 'some sort of timeline', because that term is a little bit tricky in this case, since time was yet to come into existence at the moment. I'm talking about the moment of the fall of the creature we now know as satan, but who was then known as Lucifer.

Before the earth came into existence, before time was created, the Kingdom of Heaven existed already. Although there are parts of the Bible that speak about heaven, the Word doesn't tell us much about what happened before the earth and time were created. But what we do know is that there was a time when everything was perfect and in alignment with God. It was the time when satan was still called Lucifer, which means 'Light bearer' or 'shining one'. Later he is even referred to as the 'son of the morning', because of the shining countenance he had. According to the Septuagint, the Greek Old Testament, it can also be translated as 'bringer of dawn' and 'morning star'.

As you may or may not know, God's Kingdom is extremely structured. Each and every creature has his specific task and purpose. The creature that was then known as Lucifer, was second in command in the Kingdom of Heaven. He was the second highest in rank, with only God above him. The prophet Ezekiel describes that situation in the part of the Bible that mentions the first Anointing in the 'timeline'.

You were the seal of perfection, full of wisdom and perfect in beauty. You were in Eden, the garden of God; Every precious stone was your covering: The sardius, topaz, and diamond, beryl, onyx, and jasper, sapphire,

turquoise, and emerald with gold. The workmanship of your timbrels and pipes was prepared for you on the day you were created. You were the anointed cherub who covers; I established you; You were on the holy mountain of God; You walked back and forth in the midst of fiery stones. You were perfect in your ways from the day you were created, till iniquity was found in you.
Ezekiel 28:13-15

The creature that was once described as Lucifer, had a heavenly body that was a musical instrument for worship. He was the worship leader of heaven. Notice that he wasn't 'a cherub' or 'one of the cherubs', but he was 'the only cherub'. More than that, he was 'the anointed cherub', pointing out the kind of enormous authority that he had. The fact that he was anointed, was already shown in his name, in his identity. To be anointed means 'shining', 'richness', 'fat', 'fruitful', 'oily', 'glowing', 'brightness', as one who carries the Light and radiates it. But it also stands for dedication, being set apart for God, selected by God and appointed by God. Most of these meanings can be found in the name and identity of Lucifer.

God never bypasses His authority structures. Only one who is higher in rank, higher in authority, can appoint someone, up to the level of himself, but never higher. Since there was no other equal to Lucifer, he was the only anointed cherub. There was only One Who could have anointed and appointed Lucifer to his position as cherub and second in command. That Person was God Himself. And that shows the origin of the Anointing, for it comes forth from God Himself. It is His idea, His initiative and His authority. As we can see in the Bible, that situation went very well at first. Lucifer became the seal of perfection, was full of wisdom, perfect in beauty and radiated the Light of God, as his (former) name suggests. Until iniquity was found in him.

Promotion in God's Kingdom can only be achieved by humbling ourselves. For each and every one who humbles himself, shall be exalted. Likewise, everyone who exalts himself, will be humbled. Lucifer saw his own beauty, considered his wisdom and authority, and he found his position no longer good enough. He wanted more. He wanted to be equal to God. He wanted to be God. He must have felt that he 'deserved' it. His exact thoughts are mentioned in the book of Isaiah.

"I will ascend into heaven, I will exalt my throne above the stars of God; I will also sit on the mount of the congregation on the farthest sides of the north; I will ascend above the heights of the clouds, I will be like the Most High."
Isaiah 14:13-14

Here we see the desire to be independent of God, which is the sin of pride, the biggest danger for each and every creature. And so he began his evil plan of rebellion against God, along with one third of all the angels, which is surprisingly much. He really thought that he had a chance of winning. That level of foolishness can hardly be expressed in words. And how great was his fall.

How you are fallen from heaven, o Lucifer, son of the morning! How you are cut down to the ground, you who weakened the nations!
Isaiah 14:12

By the abundance of your trading you became filled with violence within, and you sinned; Therefore I cast you as a profane thing out of the mountain of God; and I destroyed you, O covering cherub, from the midst of the fiery stones. Your heart was lifted up because of your beauty; you corrupted your wisdom for the sake of your splendor; I cast you to the ground, I laid you before kings, that they might gaze at you. You defiled your sanctuaries by the multitude of your iniquities, by the iniquity of your trading; therefore I brought fire from your midst; it devoured you, and I turned you to ashes upon the earth in the sight of all who saw you. All who knew you among the peoples are astonished at you; you have become a horror, and shall be no more forever.
Ezekiel 28:16-19

Most Bible translations do not cover this part good enough. It actually goes a bit further then it is described here. Literally it says "There is no you until eon". The depth of that ruling can hardly be imagined. It is the most intense and profound form of humiliation possible. Because of this ruling:

- Lucifer was banned from the presence of God forever;
- Lucifer was humiliated and defeated in the sight of all living creatures;
- Lucifer's beautiful body was destroyed by God's fire;
- By the ruling "There is no you until eon", God took his name away;
- Because his name was taken away, his identity was taken away;
- Because his name and identity were taken away, he lost all his authority;
- Because of all of this, he was stripped of the Anointing.

How great is such a fall! From second in command in the Kingdom of Heaven, from the Anointed Cherub, to one big zero, a nobody, a creature whose name and identity are not even acknowledged by the Almighty God. That is what it means when God tells you that there is no you. It is the most intense form of rejection possible. Because God stripped him of his name, I shall also no longer name it from this point, and refer to him as satan. But notice that the literal translation does not say 'forever', but 'until eon'. That means that satan will gain power and authority again at some point.

An eon is a time indicator, like a year, decade, century etc. However, an eon is the highest form of time indication. Yet it has no defined duration (known to man). An eon is a series of eras, which are appointed and measured by God. Only He knows when one eon ends and when the next will start. However, in this case we do know with what it will start. We know that given identity also gives authority. When mankind fell for sin, satan gained power of the earth. In 2 Corinthians 4:4 he is also called the 'god of the eon'. But he has no power to overcome the saints! That means that he doesn't have his full authority back yet, although the Bible tells us about a moment when that will happen.

It was granted to him to make war with the saints and to overcome them. And authority was given him over every tribe, tongue, and nation. All who dwell on the earth will worship him, whose names have not been written in the Book of Life of the Lamb slain from the foundation of the world.
Revelation 13:7-8

This is why the Word says that he is no more until eon. It speaks about the eon to come, where he will gain power one more time. But although he will gain power, he will never be anointed by divine Anointing anymore and his destiny is already set.

The devil, who deceived them, was cast into the lake of fire and brimstone where the beast and the false prophet are. And they will be tormented day and night forever and ever.
Revelation 20:10

Since the moment that satan fell from heaven, God never created or appointed anyone like him again. Instead He created, appointed and Anointed two cherubs, equal in perfection, equal in beauty, equal in authority and equal in wisdom. Neither can boast about their perfection or anything else, because there is always someone just like their self, right in front of them. As you can see in the image of the mercy seat, that is on the ark of the covenant (or testimony), these two anointed cherubs are next to the throne of God, facing one another and covering the glory of God.

The use of Anointing Oil and Anointing proceeded from heaven to the earth, from the moment man was created. The Bible makes no actual mention that this was from the moment of creation, but when we look at the situation in heaven and when we connect the dots, then it seems obvious. Let me make it clear that this cannot be accepted as the truth, since it can't be tested. But we can accept it as a possible scenario, since the Bible makes no mention about this. The garden of Eden was a place that existed and exists in heaven as well. The garden that God created on earth was an image of the one in heaven, just like there is an existing Jerusalem on earth and an existing Jerusalem in heaven, that will one day replace the existing Jerusalem. From Zachariah 4 and Revelation 11, we know that there are olive trees in the garden of heaven and that they serve the purpose of Anointing and Light.

Another remarkable thing is that when the dove returned to Noah, after the great flood, the first thing it brought back was an olive leaf. Because of that event, the olive leaf has become a commonly accepted symbol of peace and prosperity. After that, God told Noah to be fruitful and multiply, just as He had told Adam, right before He placed him in the garden of Eden. Several sources even go as far as naming the olive leaf a leaf from the tree of Life, although many of these sources cannot really be considered as reliable. In theory it would be possible, because the Bible defines: "the fruit tree that yields fruit according to its kind, whose seed is in itself" (Genesis 1:11). This means that the olive could have been the fruit from the tree of Life, since it also has "seed in itself" and grows on a tree. But again, the sources aren't really reliable and the Bible makes no mention of what sort of fruit it was that grew on the tree of Life, although multitudes of Christians still believe it was an apple, which most certainly is not defined anywhere and thus is also based upon an assumption.

In many cases it is known that some situations were not described or that details were not mentioned in the Bible, because it was such a common use in those times, that it was the obvious thing for the people of that time. That might be the case here as well. It is remarkable that at some point the use of Anointing Oil suddenly appears out of nothing. That is the moment when Jacob Anointed Bethel (Genesis 28:18), which takes the second place in our 'timeline'. The Word does not mention where the use came from, but as we read the story, it seems like it was already a common use and that Jacob wanted to respond to that event in a proper way. That was the event where Jacob was renamed to Israel. Again God said: "Be fruitful and multiply".

Then God appeared to Jacob again, when he came from Padan Aram, and blessed him. And God said to him, "Your name is Jacob; your name shall not be called Jacob anymore, but Israel shall be your name." So He called his name Israel. Also God said to him: "I am God Almighty. Be fruitful and multiply; a nation and a company of nations shall proceed from you, and kings shall come from your body. The land which I gave Abraham and Isaac I give to you; and to your descendants after you I give this land." Then God went up from him in the place where He talked with him. So Jacob set up a pillar in the place where He talked with him, a pillar of stone; and he poured a drink offering on it, and he poured oil on it. And Jacob called the name of the place where God spoke with him, Bethel.

Genesis 35:9-15

After that, the Word doesn't mention the use of Anointing Oil again, until God established the law, in the book of Exodus. However, according to the Jewish Encyclopedia, the Egyptian hieroglyphs do show evidence that Anointing Oil must have been used during the time that Joseph reigned over Egypt and in the time afterwards.

CHAPTER 2

THE USE OF OIL AND FRAGRANCE IN THE TABERNACLE

As we know, the oil comes from the olive and the olive from the olive tree, the source of the oil. The next place in our 'timeline' is taken by the place where God established the law of the Sabbaths. It is the third time where the Bible makes mention of the oil, and in this case it starts with the source of the oil. First the Israelites received the law regarding the use of their land, their vineyards and their olive groves. They were commanded to use their land, vineyards and olive groves for six years, and then to let it rest and lie fallow in the seventh year. Then God continues by establishing the seventh day of the week as the Sabbath. So there is a Sabbath year for the land, the vineyards and the olive groves, but a Sabbath day for the people.

Six years you shall sow your land and gather in its produce, but the seventh year you shall let it rest and lie fallow, that the poor of your people may eat; and what they leave, the beasts of the field may eat. In like manner you shall do with your vineyard and your olive grove. Six days you shall do your work, and on the seventh day you shall rest, that your ox and your donkey may rest, and the son of your female servant and the stranger may be refreshed.
Exodus 23:10-12

But what many people do not realize is that God didn't stop there. He added something to it:

And in all that I have said to you, be circumspect and make no mention of the name of other gods, nor let it be heard from your mouth.
Exodus 23:13

So these commandments were so valued by and important to God, that He didn't even want the names of other gods to be mentioned. That was a learning experience for me, because when I read this, I immediately saw myself in conversations about other religions, where I often mentioned the names of these gods. As we've learned in the previous chapter, a name is a form of acknowledgment and authority. By calling the name of another god, we acknowledge that god, which is a form of idol worship. That was the reason why God took the identity of satan away, when satan fell from heaven. To emphasize all of this, God did not only make this a covenant, He made it a blood covenant.

And Moses took the blood, sprinkled it on the people, and said, "This is the blood of the covenant which the Lord has made with you according to all these words."
Exodus 24:8

A few verses further the Bible tells us something about the appearance of God, which is quite interesting in the light of this study.

The sight of the glory of the Lord was like a consuming fire on the top of the mountain in the eyes of the children of Israel.
Exodus 24:17

As you may remember, to be anointed means 'shining', 'richness', 'fat', 'fruitful', 'oily', 'glowing', 'brightness', as one who carries the Light and radiates it. This gives such a beautiful image of the Source of our Anointing, God Himself. The One Who radiates Light, Purity and Holiness. He is the Source of all the commandments that were given to the Israelites, a special people whom God Himself selected. We must never forget that God choose this people, this nation, and that He will never bypass the Jewish people, nor that He will go back on His promised to them. Without that people and nation, we would never have our Savior and Messiah, Jesus Christ. They have always played a big role in history, in the present and God has a role for them in the future as well. The nation of Israel and the Jewish people are so very significant in God's sight. To dismiss anything of this significance or importance is one of the biggest mistakes the Church can make (and has made). It is like erasing our own history and all the promises of God along with it. We are the ones who are added. The root carries us, not the other way around.

While being in the presence of God, Moses received many instructions from the Lord. The first instruction was to bring God an offering. Not just any offering was to be accepted, but only from those who would give with a willing heart, which shows the importance of our heart and attitude when we offer something to God. Among the things that were to be offered were:

Oil for the light, and spices for the anointing oil and for the sweet incense.
Exodus 25:6

Notice that people can only give what they have. Since they were in the dessert at that time, they must have taken all the materials along with them from Egypt. Also notice that God asked for oil for the light, but not for the Anointing Oil. This suggests that they already had and used Anointing Oil. I think that these were unscented anointing oils, especially since God asked for spices for the Holy Anointing Oil at a later time (Exodus 35:28), but it also could have been both scented and unscented.

Oil and fragrances had a big role in the Tabernacle. To begin with, all the items in the Tabernacle were Anointed with the Holy Anointing Oil, including the tents and the garments of the priests. We'll talk more about that later on, but there were four items that had an ongoing role, being the golden lampstand, the showbread, the altar of incense and, of course, the Holy Anointing Oil.

THE GOLDEN LAMPSTAND: LIGHT
Contrary to what many people believe, the golden lampstand never was, is or shall be a 'candlestick'. We may use a candlestick as an image of the golden lampstand, but the original lampstand did not contain candles. It contained oil lamps. The golden lampstand was positioned in the Holy Place, at the left side, when you entered. It was made from pure gold, with one solid stem and six tubes coming out of it, three on each side. There are several symbolisms for the lampstand, but one of them is that Jesus Christ is the stem, as is mentioned in the book of John.

I am the vine, you are the branches. He who abides in Me, and I in him,

bears much fruit; for without Me you can do nothing.
John 15:5

The number six represents the number of man, equal to the six branches of the lampstand. Without that stem, the branches would not be able to stand or to hold their lights. They would fall. The number seven represents divine completeness, showing that Jesus Christ is the One Who makes us complete and Who makes us able to stand. Without Him we can do nothing.

You shall make seven lamps for it, and they shall arrange its lamps so that they give light in front of it.
Exodus 25:37

And you shall command the children of Israel that they bring you pure oil of pressed olives for the light, to cause the lamp to burn continually. In the tabernacle of meeting, outside the veil which is before the Testimony, Aaron and his sons shall tend it from evening until morning before the Lord. It shall be a statute forever to their generations on behalf of the children of Israel.
Exodus 27:20-21

This is still true today. The golden lampstand in heaven still is a statute for the generations, on behalf of the children of Israel. First for Israel, then for the gentiles, who are added (grafted) to God's people.

For if the firstfruit is holy, the lump is also holy; and if the root is holy, so are the branches. And if some of the branches were broken off, and you, being a wild olive tree, were grafted in among them, and with them became a partaker of the root and fatness of the olive tree, do not boast against the branches. But if you do boast, remember that you do not support the root, but the root supports you.
Romans 11:16-18

The lamps on the golden lampstand were to burn continually and burned on pure olive oil. The mention of pure olive oil does not point to the absence of fragrance oils, but at the type of olive oil that was to be used. It needed to be pure olive oil, which we know as virgin oil today. It means that it needed to be the best quality possible, coming from the first pressing. Although there is not much mentioned about fragrances in the oil for the Light, there is one verse that makes mention of it.

and spices and oil for the light, for the anointing oil, and for the sweet incense.
Exodus 35:28

The fragrant olive oil was the fuel for the lamps. As we will explain later in this study, the olive oil is an image of the Holy Spirit and represents the presence of the Holy Spirit in us. But the presence of this fuel is not visible from the outside, until the lamps start to burn. And just as the priest was to fill these lamps with oil each day, so that the lamps could burn continually, so our High Priest in heaven continually fills us with His Holy Spirit, so that we can burn continually.

Then Jesus spoke to them again, saying, "I am the light of the world. He who follows Me shall not walk in darkness, but have the light of life."
John 8:12

The life of our Messiah, Jesus Christ, was and is the ultimate blueprint for the Christian life. Darkness is simply the absence of Light, like evil is the absence of God. By coming to this earth, one of the things that Jesus did was bringing the Light of God with Him, along with that great promise that those who follow Him will never walk in darkness again, but will have the light of Life. The Light of life Jesus talked about was and is the Light of Jesus Himself, for He is the Way, the Truth and the Life.

"You are the light of the world. A city that is set on a hill cannot be hidden. Nor do they light a lamp and put it under a basket, but on a lampstand, and it gives light to all who are in the house. Let your light so shine before men, that they may see your good works and glorify your Father in heaven.
Matthew 5:14-16

Following in the footsteps of Jesus, having the Holy Spirit in us, and His fire to set us ablaze, we become the light of the world as well. The image of this is that the people around us may see the light that we spread, which is the Light of Jesus. That they may see and know Him and glorify our Father in heaven.

THE SHOWBREAD: FELLOWSHIP

The table with the showbread (or the 'bread of presence') could be found at the right side, when you entered the Holy Place, right across from the golden lampstand. The table contained twelve loaves of bread, representing the twelve tribes of Israel. Every week, on the Sabbath, freshly baked bread was placed on the table. The old bread was removed and eaten by the priests. On top of the stacks of showbread was pure frankincense (not mixed with oil or anything else).

And you shall put pure frankincense on each row, that it may be on the bread for a memorial, an offering made by fire to the Lord.
Leviticus 24:7

The frankincense symbolizes our prayers and worship, which can also simply be explained as us talking to God. Eating together was and is considered as an act of fellowship and friendship, a form of unity. The image of the showbread shows God's willingness and desire to have fellowship with His people. In other words, it shows His desire to talk back to us, to have a relationship with us. The fact that many people lived and live in sin does not change that fact. He desires for all to be saved and to have fellowship with every human being.

Eating with someone unholy, like the tax collectors and prostitutes, was considered to be a shame and disgrace. Yet this was what Jesus was doing while He was walking on earth. The showbread was positioned in the Holy Place, a place that was only accessible to the priests. Jesus referred to Himself as this bread.

And Jesus said to them, "I am the bread of life. He who comes to Me shall never hunger, and he who believes in Me shall never thirst."
John 6:35

I am the bread of life. Your fathers ate the manna in the wilderness, and

are dead. This is the bread which comes down from heaven, that one may eat of it and not die. I am the living bread which came down from heaven. If anyone eats of this bread, he will live forever; and the bread that I shall give is My flesh, which I shall give for the life of the world.
John 6:48-51

By saying this, Jesus Christ showed the deep desire of God to have not only fellowship with the priests, but with ordinary people as well. He came for all.

THE ALTAR OF INCENSE: PRAYER AND WORSHIP

The altar of incense was the third item that stood in the Holy Place. When you entered the Holy Place and walked between the golden lampstand (on your left side) and the table of showbread (on your right side), towards the veil that separated the Holy Place from the Holy of Holies, the altar of incense was positioned in the middle, before the veil. This was one of the two altars. The first was the bronze altar, which was positioned in the courtyard and meant for the animal sacrifices. The altar of incense was the exact same model, but a fifth of the size of the bronze altar and positioned in the Holy Place. This altar was overlaid with pure gold. It was not allowed to sacrifice blood on this altar, although some of the blood of the sacrifices that were made on the bronze altar, was applied to the horns of the altar of incense, as an anointing with blood.

In a spiritual way, the altar of incense represent the prayers and worship of the saints, as can be seen in the book of Revelation.

Now when He had taken the scroll, the four living creatures and the twenty-four elders fell down before the Lamb, each having a harp, and golden bowls full of incense, which are the prayers of the saints.
Revelation 5:8

Then another angel, having a golden censer, came and stood at the altar. He was given much incense, that he should offer it with the prayers of all the saints upon the golden altar which was before the throne. And the smoke of the incense, with the prayers of the saints, ascended before God from the angel's hand.

Revelation 8:3-4

It is likely that oil was used on the altar of incense as well, as is suggested in Exodus 30:35 and Exodus 35:28.

THE HOLY ANOINTING OIL: EMPOWERMENT

Last but not least, there is the Holy Anointing Oil. This was not an anointing oil like any other fragrance oil that was used among the Israelites. It was a special oil, made by the composition that God Himself provided. The use of it speaks of empowerment, to consecrate items and people.

With it you shall anoint the tabernacle of meeting and the ark of the Testimony; the table and all its utensils, the lampstand and its utensils, and the altar of incense; the altar of burnt offering with all its utensils, and the laver and its base. You shall consecrate them, that they may be most holy; whatever touches them must be holy. And you shall anoint Aaron and his sons, and consecrate them, that they may minister to Me as priests.
Exodus 30:26-30

CHAPTER 3

THE EXODUS OIL

Throughout the last years I have heard so many people say that they believe that the use of Anointing Oil is prohibited, or at least limited to the Anointing of the sick. Some say this based on the things that God said about the Holy Anointing Oil. Others use the oil so freely, that they believe that every composition or recipe can be used for every purpose. It is always good and wise to know what the Word of God actually says about something.

When it comes to Holy Oil, the Bible makes mention of two recipes. The first is the recipe of the Holy Anointing Oil, which was liquid, the other is the recipe of the Holy Incense, which was most likely also made with oil, but less liquid and like a more solid substance. Both recipes were and are considered holy and most holy. Both recipes come with a serious warning, so the fact that many people are very careful in regard to the use of this Anointing Oil is very suitable.

THE RECIPE OF HOLY ANOINTING OIL
Also take for yourself quality spices—five hundred shekels of liquid myrrh, half as much sweet-smelling cinnamon (two hundred and fifty shekels), two hundred and fifty shekels of sweet-smelling cane, five hundred shekels of cassia, according to the shekel of the sanctuary, and a hin of olive oil.
Exodus 30:23-24

THE RECIPE OF THE HOLY INCENSE
Take sweet spices, stacte and onycha and galbanum, and pure frankincense with these sweet spices; there shall be equal amounts of each.
Exodus 30:34

These are the recipes that are never to be used again. But to conclude that God is talking about the use of Anointing Oil in general is a mistake. That was not what He said. Some assume that when they use Anointing Oil, or an Anointing Oil containing any of the fragrances mentioned, that the curse of God will become effective in their life. This is not true either.

In regard to the Holy Anointing Oil, God said: "This shall be a holy anointing oil to Me throughout your generations. It shall not be poured on man's flesh; nor shall you make any other like it, according to its composition. It is holy, and it shall be holy to you. Whoever compounds any like it, or whoever puts any of it on an outsider, shall be cut off from his people." (Exodus 30:31-33)

Here God says that the existing Holy Anointing Oil may never be used on man's flesh. That leaves room for the Anointing of items and/or garments, but not for human beings. That is assuming that this Anointing Oil (that was made at that moment) still exists somewhere, which I dare not to say. If it does, it is most likely not accessible to any of us, so that solves that problem. The other thing God says is that this Anointing Oil is never to be made again, but notice that God adds something very important to it: "according to its composition". In other words, you may make Anointing Oil with any of the separate ingredients of the Holy Anointing Oil, but never in the exact same recipe that was used for the Holy Anointing Oil. He who does that anyway, shall be cut off from his people. And yes, that is a curse that will become effective for anyone who does that. So it is very justified to be cautious on this area.

In regard to the Holy Incense, God said: "It shall be most holy to you. But as for the incense which you shall make, you shall not make any for yourselves, according to its composition. It shall be to you holy for the Lord. Whoever makes any like it, to smell it, he shall be cut off from his people." (Exodus 30: 36-37).

Here it even goes a step further. He who makes this recipe, even if it's only to smell it, shall be cut off from his people. The Holy Anointing Oil is called 'holy', but the Holy Incense is called 'Most Holy'. No matter what kind of product you want to make, when you use this recipe as your fragrance, the curse will become effective immediately. This is talking about the fragrance alone. So there are two recipes that are not to be made again, not just one.

Some believe that the use of these recipes is justified and that nothing will happen to them, because Jesus became a curse and carried all the consequences of it at the cross. While it is true that Jesus dealt with each and every curse, it only applies to those who are in line with the Word of God. Doing something that goes against the will of God is always considered a sin. Just like you can't commit adultery or murder without facing the consequences in the natural and in the spiritual, it is also impossible to violate this law without facing the consequences. Forgiveness is only for those who admit with their mouths and in their hearts that they have committed a sin and are in need of forgiveness, not for those who use the grace of God as an excuse to freely commit sins.

Sometimes the fear of making mistakes or to commit sin becomes so big, that we rather choose for a 'safe path', then to explore any more of what God has to offer. We tend to look for security and safety by staying away from the things we don't understand. Yes, there is such a thing as the fear of the Lord, which is the beginning of wisdom. But the fear of making mistakes is not a part of that fear. Fear of making mistakes is a bad counselor. The only real security can be found in the Word of God. That is the place where you can be really safe.

Not using Anointing Oil, out of fear of violating God's commandments from Exodus 30, is like not praying, because you might pray a prayer that is not according to His will. It is like not believing, because you might believe wrong. In those cases, we get stuck in legalism. The power behind legalism will always prevent you from doing things for the Lord, from the fear of doing it wrong. That doesn't make us safe or free, it makes us a spiritual prisoner. True safety and freedom can be found in our Lord and Messiah, Jesus Christ, for He is the Living Word. And His promise to us still stands today:

If you abide in My word, you are My disciples indeed. And you shall know the truth, and the truth shall make you free.
John 8:31-32

What is the key? Abide in His Word. If you're not sure if something is right, abide in His Word. If you're not sure what to do next, abide in His

Word. Open the Word of God, search for the answers. Then you can know for sure. Our first question should always be: "What does the Word of God have to say about this situation?". It most certainly shouldn't be what someone else has to say about it. Sure, you can listen to the advice of people, but never accept any of that advice as the truth, until you are able to confirm it from the Word of God. That is including this study.

As for the use of Anointing Oil, you can find clear answers in the Bible. In the Bible verses I've just given you, you can see that the Exodus Anointing Oil and Holy Incense are specific recipes. The Word does not say "Thou shall not use Anointing Oil", it says "Don't use these recipes". The book of Exodus also does not put any restrictions on who is allowed to use Anointing Oil. It puts restrictions on who is allowed to use the Holy Anointing Oil and the Holy Incense, that was made for that time and for the service in the Tabernacle. It also puts restrictions on producing those same recipes again. But each and every other recipe for Anointing Oil and fragrances are still free to use. The question of who is allowed to use all these other Anointing Oils will be answered later on in this study. That answer may surprise you.

CHAPTER 4
THE IMAGE OF ANOINTING OIL

The Anointing and the use of Anointing Oil have a deep spiritual meaning. And with spiritual I mean Spiritual. It is not 'an' image, but 'the' image of empowerment by the Holy Spirit. It is a symbol of the indwelling of the Holy Spirit in man. The anointed ones are also referred to as sons of oil, the ones with a shining countenance, glowing ones, bright ones and "God's great ones". The question that remains is, of course, what it should express? Whenever I read these terms and descriptions of anointing, I always have to think back to these verses:

The sight of the glory of the Lord was like a consuming fire on the top of the mountain in the eyes of the children of Israel.
Exodus 24:17

Now it was so, when Moses came down from Mount Sinai (and the two tablets of the Testimony were in Moses' hand when he came down from the mountain), that Moses did not know that the skin of his face shone while he talked with Him. So when Aaron and all the children of Israel saw Moses, behold, the skin of his face shone, and they were afraid to come near him.
Exodus 34:29-30

He was transfigured before them. His face shone like the sun, and His clothes became as white as the light.
Matthew 17:2

Whenever the glory and holiness of God becomes manifest, this is what happens. I have heard and seen that events like these are still happening in these days, just like the fact that the miracles of the Bible are also still happening in these days. Yes, all of them, and more. God has never changed. Jesus never changed. If we move in the same faith as the disciples, if we preach the same gospel as they did and if we pay the same price they paid, all the signs and miracles that followed them, will follow us as well. Not from our own strength or by our own efforts, but by the power of our best Friend, Comforter and Companion, the Holy Spirit. All things are really possible, if we have faith.

When people used anointing oil, their countenance started to shine and glow from the oil. That is the image of God with us, an image of being in the constant presence of His glory and holiness. Moses had to climb a mountain to be in the presence of God. Jesus is God, but climbed a mountain anyway, to take His disciples with Him, to witness the glory and holiness. When the outpouring of the Holy Spirit took place, this went to a whole new level. From that moment it was not just God with us, but it became God in us as well, like God had intended it to be. It can be compared with the oil lamps, which are filled with oil and are burning and shining light. Likewise we can become filled with the Holy Spirit and burn for Jesus, shining His Light for the nations.

The image of the anointing and the Holy Spirit was already visible with the prophets, kings and priests of Israel in the Old Testament. It was a prelude of what was about to happen in the future. Whenever a prophet, king or priest was anointed, the empowerment by the Holy Spirit followed. This can, among others, be seen at the anointing of Saul and David.

Then Samuel took a flask of oil and poured it on his head, and kissed him and said: "Is it not because the Lord has anointed you commander over His inheritance? (Verse 1)
Then the Spirit of the Lord will come upon you, and you will prophesy with them and be turned into another man. (Verse 6)
1 Samuel 10:1, 6

Then Samuel took the horn of oil and anointed him in the midst of his brothers; and the Spirit of the Lord came upon David from that day forward. So Samuel arose and went to Ramah.
1 Samuel 16:13

The empowerment by the Holy Spirit was not something that happened to ordinary people in those days. It happened only with prophets, kings and priests. So the fact that Jesus was empowered by the Holy Spirit was something remarkable for the people of that time. At one point Jesus quoted a passage from the book of Isaiah, chapter 61, which was a well-known passage for the people of that time and place. It is that passage that clearly shows the connection between the anointing and the Holy Spirit. He said: "The Spirit of the Lord is upon Me". Directly afterwards He tells why: "because of which He has anointed Me".

The Spirit of the Lord is upon Me, because (of which) He has anointed Me to preach the gospel to the poor; He has sent Me to heal the brokenhearted, to proclaim liberty to the captives and recovery of sight to the blind, to set at liberty those who are oppressed; To proclaim the acceptable year of the Lord.
Luke 4:18-19

How God anointed Jesus of Nazareth with the Holy Spirit and with power, who went about doing good and healing all who were oppressed by the devil, for God was with Him.
Acts 10:38

Some translations say that the Spirit was on Jesus because He was Anointed, but the remarkable thing is that, in this case, it is the other way around. It originally says that the Spirit was on Jesus, because of which He was Anointed. As you can see in the Old Testament, the Holy Spirit came after someone was anointed by order of the Lord (not by their own initiative). But Jesus, the Christ, the Anointed One, already had and has the identity of 'being Anointed'. He is God, the Source of the Anointing! Not only does this show the clear connection between Anointing and the Holy Spirit, it also shows the aim of the Anointing, which was and is to preach the gospel, to heal the brokenhearted, to proclaim liberty to the captives, to recover the sight of the blind (physical and spiritual!), to liberate the oppressed and to proclaim the acceptable year of the Lord.

All earthly materials and all the people of this earth are not naturally holy. When the Tabernacle was built, none of the materials were holy. The people who were about to become priests, were not yet holy. Everything became holy, because of the Anointing. Whatever was Anointed became holy from that moment on. Here's an example of that principal.

And you shall take the anointing oil, and anoint the tabernacle and all that is in it; and you shall hallow it and all its utensils, and it shall be holy. You shall anoint the altar of the burnt offering and all its utensils, and consecrate the altar. The altar shall be most holy.
Exodus 40:9-10

So holiness came because of the Anointing. In the same way, it is the Holy Spirit Who makes us holy, because of the Anointing of Jesus. It is by His Word, through His Spirit, that we are changed to holiness. The more time we spent in His Word, with alertness for what the Holy Spirit wants to teach us through it, the more we are transformed to holiness. There was a season in my life where the Holy Spirit told me the same thing over and over again, every day, several times a day, for months. The thing He told me was this: "Only the Word of God has the power to change you." It was because of that Word that my love for the Word of God started to grow even more. I started to see, recognize and acknowledge its value. It is a message so simple, yet it was probably one of the most powerful messages that He has ever taught me.

How different was this in the life of Jesus. He had no need for the Anointing to make Him holy. He already was holy. For that reason the Anointing was on Him. When He quoted the passage from Isaiah 61, "The Spirit of the Lord is upon Me, because (of which) He has anointed Me", that was a revelation of Himself as the promised Messiah. In those times the title "messiah" was not exclusively reserved for the Savior. As mentioned before, the word "messiah" means "anointed one". It was a title that was used for all the prophets, who were also called messiah's in those days and throughout the whole Old Testament. Even though the kings and priests were anointed as well, the term messiah was only used to address the prophets. That was probably the reason why so many people addressed Jesus as a messiah.

When Jesus came into the region of Caesarea Philippi, He asked His disciples, saying, "Who do men say that I, the Son of Man, am?" So they said, "Some say John the Baptist, some Elijah, and others Jeremiah or one of the prophets."
Matthew 16:13-14

Most likely they said: "one of the messiah's" or "one of the christ's". As you may remember, the term "messiah" is a Hebrew word, which translates as "christ" in Greek. Addressing Jesus with that title basically only says that He is an Anointed, like the prophets were Anointed as well. So although calling Him Christ or Messiah is an acknowledgement of the Anointing of God, it is not more than that. There are other religions, including the bigger religions like the islam, who are also acknowledging Him as Christ. That may sound confusing, but the difference lies in the statement that Peter did, when Jesus asked them who they said He was (and is).

Simon Peter answered and said, "You are the Christ, the Son of the living God." Jesus answered and said to him, "Blessed are you, Simon Bar-Jonah, for flesh and blood has not revealed this to you, but My Father who is in heaven. And I also say to you that you are Peter, and on this rock I will build My church, and the gates of Hades shall not prevail against it. And I will give you the keys of the kingdom of heaven, and whatever you bind on earth will be bound in heaven, and whatever you loose on earth will be loosed in heaven."
Matthew 16:16-20

Although several religions acknowledge Jesus as Christ, only Christianity acknowledges Him as the Son of the living God. No other religion will acknowledge Him as the Son of God. That is a big difference. Although the prophets were called "messiah's" or "christ's", they were all ordinary people, naturally unclean and unholy, but made clean and holy because of the Anointing. There was only One Who could say that He already was clean and holy, because of which God Anointed Him. That person is Jesus. The only One Who lived His entire life without sin. That didn't make Him a messiah, it made Him THE MESSIAH, the Son of the living God. And the only way to come to that revelation and acknowledgement, is by the revelation of the Father, through the Holy Spirit.

Calling Jesus THE MESSIAH is calling Him "God's greatest One", which He is. It is because of His Anointing and because of His sacrifice, that the presence of God left the temple and tore the veil, to make His indwelling in man, by His Holy Spirit. That is the image of the spiritual Anointing and what Anointing with Anointing Oil symbolizes. It is the Holy Spirit in us, as the seal of our salvation.

In Him you also trusted, after you heard the word of truth, the gospel of your salvation; in whom also, having believed, you were sealed with the Holy Spirit of promise, who is the guarantee of our inheritance until the redemption of the purchased possession, to the praise of His glory.
Ephesians 1:13-14

As I always say in all of my teachings, the aim of God is always to save, to heal, to deliver and to restore. So whenever the Holy Spirit starts to work in and through us, the fruits will always align with salvation, healing, deliverance and restoration. Everything and everyone that works against those things, is working against God, against the Anointing, against the sacrifice of Jesus and for the agenda of the enemy. But when the Holy Spirit really is in control, and when the Church totally submits to God and let Him have His way, then you will see it by the fruits. A lack of the fruits means a lack of the Spirit. A beautiful image of the restoration of God's people can be seen in 2 Chronicles, where the people of Judah were released and restored to honor, by the Anointing.

Then the men who were designated by name rose up and took the captives, and from the spoil they clothed all who were naked among them, dressed them and gave them sandals, gave them food and drink, and anointed them.
2 Chronicles 28:15

The image of the Anointing is also seen in the prayer for healing. When someone is sick, their face does not look very happy or shining. The anointing makes the face shine again in the natural, as an image of what happens in the spiritual realm, if the prayer for healing is done from and with faith. According to the customs of that time, it is also a visible sign, showing the end of the time of mourning. The next verse is speaking about the aim of the Anointing of Jesus Christ.

To give them beauty for ashes, the oil of joy for mourning, the garment of praise for the spirit of heaviness; that they may be called trees of

righteousness, the planting of the Lord, that He may be glorified.
Isaiah 61:3

This speaks about the promise of God, to remove the spirit of mourning and heaviness, and to grant the Holy Spirit and the Holy Anointing in its place. The trees of righteousness are olive trees, having the oil of Anointing in their fruits. The oil of joy that this verse is talking about is the oil of Jesus Christ Himself, which is referred to in Hebrews 1:9. The Spirit of Jesus Christ as the oil of exultation or the oil of elation (literal translation).

You have loved righteousness and hated lawlessness; Therefore God, Your God, has anointed You with the oil of gladness more than Your companions.
Hebrews 1:9

The last image of Anointing Oil that I see is the following. No one can touch oil, without leaving traces of it on their hands. Likewise, no one can be touched by Jesus, by the Holy Spirit, by the Anointing, and leave empty handed.

CHAPTER 5

THE ANOINTING OF THE ROYAL PRIESTHOOD

When God created mankind, He didn't make a mistake. Even before He created mankind, He knew exactly how things would go. His master plan for the salvation of mankind didn't start at the birth of Jesus Christ. It had already started from the very beginning, right after Adam and Eve had fallen for sin, as if He had expected it all. The plan of salvation was activated immediately. After Cain murdered Abel in a terrible way, Adam received another son: Seth. A son in his own likeness (Genesis 5:3). From his descendants the salvation plan of God continued. From Seth to Enos, to Cainan, to Mahalaleel, to Jared, to Enoch (who walked with God and never died, because God took Him), to Methuselah, to Lamech, to Noah.

Noah was a just man, perfect in his generations. Noah walked with God (Genesis 6:9). Then the Great Flood came over the earth and killed all the descendants of Adam, except Noah and his sons, and their families. After that, the family line continued to his oldest son Shem (who covered the nakedness of his father, Genesis 9:23), all the way to Terah, the father of Abraham. God's choice for Abraham was far from random or remarkable. He Himself had prepared a perfect, holy and worthy family line, to establish and carry out His salvation plan for the world.

GOD'S ORIGINAL PLAN FOR ISRAEL
As we all know, the story of the people of Israel started with the promise God gave to Abraham. It was this promise that started to show God's intentions to save the world. God called Abraham for a purpose that was so big, that he could hardly imagine it.

Get out of your country, from your family and from your father's house, to a land that I will show you. I will make you a great nation; I will bless you and make your name great; and you shall be a blessing. I will bless those

who bless you, and I will curse him who curses you; and in you all the families of the earth shall be blessed.
Genesis 12:1-3

The people and the nation of Israel were God's original plan for the salvation of the world. As we can see in the promise that God gave to Abraham, He wanted to bless all the families of the world. Later on, in the book of Exodus, God makes a remarkable statement, in regard to the people of Israel.

You have seen what I did to the Egyptians, and how I bore you on eagles' wings and brought you to Myself. Now therefore, if you will indeed obey My voice and keep My covenant, then you shall be a special treasure to Me above all people; for all the earth is Mine. And you shall be to Me a kingdom of priests and a holy nation.' These are the words which you shall speak to the children of Israel.
Exodus 19:4-6

The remarkable thing is the fact that God said that they would be a "kingdom of priests". This was a promise God gave to the people of Israel, right before He established the law. When you were appointed as a priest, it was always to serve someone else, to act on behalf of someone else. So if God wanted to make the entire nation of Israel a kingdom of priests, then the question is: On behalf of whom? That question can be answered from God's promise to Abraham, in Genesis 12:3. He wanted to make the nation of Israel a kingdom of priests, on behalf of the rest of the world. It was all part of His big salvation plan.

For you are a holy people to the Lord your God; the Lord your God has chosen you to be a people for Himself, a special treasure above all the peoples on the face of the earth. The Lord did not set His love on you nor choose you because you were more in number than any other people, for you were the least of all peoples; but because the Lord loves you, and because He would keep the oath which He swore to your fathers, the Lord has brought you out with a mighty hand, and redeemed you from the house of bondage, from the hand of Pharaoh king of Egypt.
Deuteronomy 7:6-8

God dealt with Israel as a show case for the rest of the world. They were and are a chosen people, a special nation and a treasure to God. But they are also human beings, which means that they have the same human heart as anyone else. The kind of heart that produces all sorts of sins, just like Jesus said in Matthew 15:19. Then what was the difference? The difference was that God had shown them the road to mercy, the road to salvation. By making them a show case for the rest of the world, the world was able to see that God blessed them whenever they were obedient, and what the results would be whenever they would not obey Him. Thus God used the people of Israel to make Himself known to the world.

THE GENTILES WELCOMED AMONG GOD'S PEOPLE

We often very wrongly assume that the gentiles were first welcomed among God's people in the New Testament. This is not true. Even in the Old Testament, everyone was allowed and able to serve God, to receive salvation and to become a part of God's people.

And when a stranger dwells with you and wants to keep the Passover to the Lord, let all his males be circumcised, and then let him come near and keep it; and he shall be as a native of the land. For no uncircumcised person shall eat it. One law shall be for the native-born and for the stranger who dwells among you.
Exodus 12:48-49

The difference between now and then is the fact that back then, it was only the law that could offer them salvation. If they had committed a sin, the same rules applied to them and they had to bring an offering to receive forgiveness. An example of the acceptance of foreign people, is Ruth. She had married an Israelite, but became a widow very soon. Determined as she was, she choose to stay with her mother-in-law and declared, "Your people shall be my people, and your God, my God". Later she married with Boaz and became a part of the family line, from which Jesus would come forth.

In the New Testament it pretty soon became clear what the sacrifice of Jesus means for the rest of the world. In Acts 11, Peter talks about a vision he saw and how the Holy Spirit called him to go to a gentile man. That man had seen an angel, who told him to call for Peter. When Peter began to speak to him and his household, the Spirit fell upon them, in the same way that happened to the disciples. Then Peter concluded:

If therefore God gave them the same gift as He gave us when we believed on the Lord Jesus Christ, who was I that I could withstand God? When they heard these things they became silent; and they glorified God, saying, "Then God has also granted to the Gentiles repentance to life."
Acts 11:17-18

Therefore remember that you, once Gentiles in the flesh—who are called Uncircumcision by what is called the Circumcision made in the flesh by hands—that at that time you were without Christ, being aliens from the commonwealth of Israel and strangers from the covenants of promise, having no hope and without God in the world. But now in Christ Jesus you who once were far off have been brought near by the blood of Christ.
Ephesians 2:11-13

THE ROYAL PRIESTHOOD
While the whole nation of Israel was called by God to be a kingdom of priests, we know that that didn't happen. Only one tribe, Levi, became priests and because of the issues among the people, the other eleven tribes never became priests. Thus the world got completely out of sight, since Israel was too busy dealing with their own problems and sins. But all of that changed when Jesus came to the earth and because of His sacrifice for us.

Coming to Him as to a living stone, rejected indeed by men, but chosen by God and precious, you also, as living stones, are being built up a spiritual house, a holy priesthood, to offer up spiritual sacrifices acceptable to God through Jesus Christ. Therefore it is also contained in the Scripture, "Behold, I lay in Zion a chief cornerstone, elect, precious, and he who believes on Him will by no means be put to shame." Therefore, to you who believe, He is precious; but to those who are disobedient, "The stone which the builders rejected has become the chief cornerstone," and "A stone of stumbling and a rock of offense." They stumble, being disobedient to the word, to which they

also were appointed. But you are a chosen generation, a royal priesthood, a holy nation, His own special people, that you may proclaim the praises of Him who called you out of darkness into His marvelous light; who once were not a people but are now the people of God, who had not obtained mercy but now have obtained mercy.
1 Petrus 2:4-9

The Bible speaks about us, the believers and followers of Jesus Christ, as a holy priesthood and a royal priesthood. By His sacrifice we may now freely enter into His presence. Because we are made righteous and holy, because of His sacrifice, we are now all appointed as priests, with Jesus Christ, the Son of God, as our High Priest and King in Heaven. Because of that, the world is now back in sight. If you are a believer and follower of Jesus, then you are part of this royal priesthood.

Now how does this relate to the Anointing and the Anointing Oil? In the times of the Old and New Testament, all the people used Anointing Oil, as a sign and prophetic act of dedication to God. We will deal with that matter in the next chapter. But although they anointed themselves, and although the Anointing is a sign of the empowerment by the Holy Spirit, none of them had the Holy Spirit. That was a special Anointing that was only for the prophets, kings and priests. They were the only people who received the Holy Spirit. Not only is our priesthood proven by the fact that the Word of God says so, but also by the fact that we are empowered by the Holy Spirit. It was (and is) impossible and unthinkable that the Holy Spirit would come over ordinary people. That happens only to a special and chosen people, of which we are now part. Not only for our own sake, but for the sake of the rest of the world. When the Bible calls you a priest, which it does when you are a follower of Jesus, then that means you are a priest on behalf of the nations. So you have a task in this world, like all of us.

By no means does the Bible speak of an eternal rejection of the people and nation of Israel. I can't emphasize that enough. All these Bible verses have been abused so many times, by people who claimed that we are the 'new spiritual Israel' and that the Jews are done. It is so dangerous to make such statements and it will cause the Anointing to leave you, as is proven throughout the whole history of Israel. Remember, it is God Who chose them, they did not choose themselves. When you have a problem with this, you don't have a problem with Israel, but with God. Then your argument against Israel and the Jews is an argument against God. Yes, the Bible calls us living stones that creates a spiritual building. But never in the place of Israel or the Jews.

I say then, have they stumbled that they should fall? Certainly not! But through their fall, to provoke them to jealousy, salvation has come to the Gentiles. Now if their fall is riches for the world, and their failure riches for the Gentiles, how much more their fullness!
Romans 11:11-12

Instead something much more beautiful happened. The gentiles, who have in no way been prepared for holiness in their family lines, were offered the opportunity to receive salvation through Jesus Christ and to be added to God's people. As branches of wild olive trees, carried by the root, yet part of the tree and the fatness of the olive tree, which is the Anointing.

For if the firstfruit is holy, the lump is also holy; and if the root is holy, so are the branches. And if some of the branches were broken off, and you, being a wild olive tree, were grafted in among them, and with them became a partaker of the root and fatness of the olive tree, do not boast against the branches. But if you do boast, remember that you do not support the root, but the root supports you.
Romans 11:16-18

There can be no priesthood or Anointing in our lives, when we reject Israel or the Jews. So if that has been what you were doing, then this is the cause of your lack of priesthood and Anointing. In that case you need to repent, which is to change your mind, to change your way of thinking, in regard to this matter. You will find that the results will be amazing.

CHAPTER 6

WHO IS ALLOWED TO USE ANOINTING OIL?

I have heard this question so many times. Who is allowed to use Anointing Oil? I have always replied to this question with the answer that everyone is allowed to use it, and I still stand by this answer. In fact, I have found so much more proof about this, while studying this topic. The personal use of Anointing Oil was a common use throughout the whole Old Testament and throughout the whole New Testament. It was a common use among the people of Israel, and later also among the Christians of the first Churches. The personal use of Anointing Oil can be found in these Bible verses.

Therefore wash yourself and anoint yourself, put on your best garment and go down to the threshing floor; but do not make yourself known to the man until he has finished eating and drinking.
Ruth 3:3

And wine that makes glad the heart of man, Oil to make his face shine, and bread which strengthens man's heart.
Psalm 104:15

Let your garments always be white, and let your head lack no oil.
Ecclesiastes 9:8

But you, when you fast, anoint your head and wash your face
Matthew 6:17

All the way through the Old Testament to the New Testament, common people used Anointing Oil to Anoint themselves. In Matthew, even Jesus told His disciples to do so. Why did He tell them that? As a religious act during fasting? Absolutely not. Anointing yourself was such a common use, that all people walked around with their faces Anointed. The thing was that the Pharisees and Scribes loved to show that they were fasting, in order to receive the honor of man. They did so by putting on a sad face and by not Anointing themselves. When you didn't Anoint yourself in these times, you really stood out and the people could see that something was going on with you. It was also a common use that you didn't Anoint yourself during times of fasting, so it wasn't a strange thing to do. The Pharisees and Scribes did it in order to make it visible to the people that they were fasting. To show everyone how religious they behaved. Jesus dealt with this issue, by saying that when you are fasting, that you need to do that for our Father in heaven and not to be seen by man. Thus He commanded His disciples to act as they always did, when they were fasting. In other words, they needed to wash their faces, as they always did, and they needed to Anoint their heads, as they always did. By doing so, they looked exactly like anyone else, without anyone noticing that they were fasting. Jesus added this promise to it:

And your Father who sees in secret will reward you openly.
Matthew 6:18

The lack of Anointing was also a sign of mourning. When something terrible happened, like when someone died, then the family friends did not Anoint themselves. Everyone in their environment could see that they were in a season of mourning, by the lack of oil on their heads. Such can be seen in the following Bible verses.

And Joab sent to Tekoa and brought from there a wise woman, and said to her, "Please pretend to be a mourner, and put on mourning apparel; do not anoint yourself with oil, but act like a woman who has been mourning a long time for the dead.
2 Samuel 14:2

I ate no pleasant food, no meat or wine came into my mouth, nor did I anoint myself at all, till three whole weeks were fulfilled.
Daniel 10:3

This can also be found in the story of king David. After he had committed adultery with Bathsheba, she became pregnant and bore a son. David was then visited by the prophet Nathan, who confronted him with his sin, for which David was clearly blinded. Nathan used a parable and God opened David's eyes for his sin. He immediately pleaded guilty with the words: "I have sinned against the Lord." As a result of his attitude towards the sin, meaning his confession of pleading guilty, his life was spared by the Lord. But in those days the sacrifice of Jesus had not yet taken place, so the verdict was that his child would die, the child he had with Bathsheba. David was devastated. The child became ill and David started to plead with God for the child. He fasted and lay on the ground all night. This went on for seven days, during which he refused to eat. At the end of the seven days, the Word of the Lord came to pass and the child died. Basically he had already mourned for the child's death. But when the child had died, he saw that there was nothing more that he could do and he ended his time of mourning. As you can see in the next verse, he did so by washing himself and by anointing himself.

So David arose from the ground, washed and anointed himself, and changed his clothes; and he went into the house of the Lord and worshiped. Then he went to his own house; and when he requested, they set food before him, and he ate.
2 Samuel 12:20

By anointing himself, he showed to everyone that his time of mourning was over. It was the sign of restoration to his normal condition, emotionally and physically. Not anointing yourself is not only a sign of mourning, it is also a sign of being cursed. How? The opposite, anointing yourself, was and is a sign of the blessing and favor of God upon your life. The lack of blessing and favor is therefore a sign of a curse. This is also mentioned in Deuteronomy, where the results of a curse were mentioned.

You shall have olive trees throughout all your territory, but you shall not anoint yourself with the oil; for your olives shall drop off.
Deuteronomy 28:40

So whenever people anointed themselves, it was a prophetic act and a sign that they were doing well, while the lack of anointing showed they were mourning and felt cursed, which some were because of their disobedience to the Word of God. Once the mourning was over, or once repentance and restoration had taken place, the use of Anointing Oil was resumed. When Jesus sent out His disciples, He gave them clear instructions on what to do.

So they went out and preached that people should repent. And they cast out many demons, and anointed with oil many who were sick, and healed them.
Marc 6:12-13

They prayed for the sick and Anointed them with oil. Keep in mind that Anointing Oil was only used after it was determined that someone was healed, not while they were still sick. So what the disciples did was an act of faith, a prophetic act of declaring that their prayer was heard and that their words, spoken on behalf of Jesus, already had come to pass. They anointed the sick in faith, believing that it was already done, even before there were visible signs. And because of that faith, the sick were healed.

Although it sometimes may seem that way, Jesus Christ was in no way a rebel in the time that He walked on earth. Some may have considered Him a rebel, but the only thing He stood up against were the religious and political spirits. The people who acted from these spirits were addressed by Jesus as hypocrites. But other than that, He never stood up against the Word of God in any way. He always obeyed the Scriptures in every detail. Jesus Christ was and is the role model for every Christian, for every disciple. He showed the people what the Christian life (meaning the "Anointed Life") was like, by living it, then by telling and encouraging His followers to do the same. So when He told His disciples to Anoint themselves when they were fasting, as they always did, it can only mean that He did the exact same thing. Otherwise He would have been a hypocrite, which He is clearly not. Jesus and all His disciples, all His followers, used Anointing Oil on a daily basis, for personal use and to Anoint others.

The common personal use of Anointing Oil among Christians continued throughout the whole New Testament, in all Jewish Christian Churches and in all the Gentile Christian Churches. In the early Churches, all people brought their Anointing Oil with them to the Church services. During the service, a blessing was spoken over the Anointing Oil, after which people took it back home again, for their personal daily use. This common personal use continued until the ninth century. Around that time, the Church rituals and Church rules arose and the common personal use of Anointing Oil became less and less, until the personal use vanished completely in the ninth century. Instead, the Anointing Oil was only to be used by the Church leaders. We're talking about the early Catholic Church. The Catholic Church had established defined Anointing rites, and only for the Anointing of the sick people. What a loss. All of this took place before the Great Schism and way before the reformation. By the time those events took place, most people didn't even know about the meaning of the Anointing and the Anointing Oil, than except for the Anointing of the sick.

After the Great Schism, and a century before the Reformation, it even became worse. From that moment the Church leaders decided that the Anointing was no longer for the sick, but only for those who were about to die. So if you were sick, you had to wait until you were dying, before one of the Church leaders was even willing to come and Anoint you. After all, Church rules and Church rituals went before the Bible in that time. In some Churches that is still the case.

Then the Reformation took place and all sorts of denominations started to grow. I couldn't really find much of the history of the use of Anointing Oil in all of the denominations, but given the fact that most denominations still only use the Anointing for the sick, tells a lot. There are even many Churches who don't use Anointing Oil at all anymore. Nowadays it is mostly because of a lack of knowledge. In the sixties of the twentieth century, the Catholic Church came back on their decision in regard to the Anointing of the sick, and decided that from that moment, all the sick should be Anointed again, according to the Scriptures. From that moment the people no longer had to wait until they were about to die. However, in the majority of the Churches and denominations, the personal common use of Anointing Oil has never been restored. Again, it is a great loss for the Church.

So many people have been blinded by the tangle of Church rules and Church rituals, which are manmade and were never commanded by the Lord. There is only one safe place in this world, and that is in the Word of God. Church rules or Church rituals will never offer you any form of security. Go back to the basic, go back to the Word of God itself. Let the Word of God decide what is true and what isn't.

As for the use of Anointing Oil and the Anointing, the Word is clear. To make it easy for you, I have even included every Bible verse that speaks about the Anointing, the Anointing Oil, the Olive Trees and the Olives, at the end of this book. In that way you don't have to assume, you don't have to blindly accept this as the truth, but you can see for yourself and test it. To me, Jesus is my role model. He is the blueprint of what true Christianity should be like. If He, His disciples and all the first Churches, were using Anointing Oil for personal use, on a daily basis, then so do I. Jesus Christ is my Master. I follow His example. And I encourage you to do the same.

CHAPTER 7

THE VARIOUS TYPES OF NATURAL ANOINTING

Throughout my early years in the Church, the only thing I had seen, in regard to Anointing Oil, was how a Church leader would put a drop of oil on his finger and then applied it on someone's forehead, in the form of a cross. That happened only when people were sick. The times that I visited other Churches, it wasn't any different. Actually, in these days I still don't see much different than that, although the awareness of the Anointing Oil is growing in the Churches. As we've seen in the previous chapter, everyone is allowed to use Anointing Oil for personal use. But how do we use it? One thing is for sure. Applying a drop of oil on your finger and anointing the forehead, in the sign of a cross, is not something I was able to find backing for or confirm from the Word of God. The following descriptions are telling you about the different ways of Anointing and the prophetic meaning. We know that the Anointing itself is an image of the empowerment by the Holy Spirit, but this is speaking about the ways on Anointing, the prophetic meanings of the application of the oil.

ANOINTING BY MASHAH
This way of Anointing is to pour a little bit Anointing Oil on your hand and then to gently apply it to the whole face, in the same way that you wash your face. This first way of Anointing was the most common used and the way people used for personal Anointing and for the Anointing of the sick. Let us take a look at a few Bible verses again.

And wine that makes glad the heart of man, Oil to make his face shine, and bread which strengthens man's heart.
Psalm 104:15

Let your garments always be white, and let your head lack no oil.
Ecclesiastes 9:8

But you, when you fast, anoint your head and wash your face
Matthew 6:17

As you read the first chapters of this book, you can see that one of the meanings of the use of Anointing Oil, was to make the face shine. The prophetic meaning of this was and is the shining Light of God, Who has filled us with His oil (Holy Spirit) and Who has set us ablaze. It is an image of the glory of God in and on us. Examples of what happens when the glory of God is near, can be seen in Exodus 24:17, Exodus 34:29-30 and Matthew 17:2.

The meaning of the word 'Mashah' is 'to daub' or 'to smear', but also 'to stroke', 'to draw the hand over', 'drawn out' and 'chosen'. All together, these meanings show the total picture of Anointing. While reading this, the Holy Spirit brought something back in my memory, being the part in the Bible where God covered Moses with His hand.

And the Lord said, "Here is a place by Me, and you shall stand on the rock. So it shall be, while My glory passes by, that I will put you in the cleft of the rock, and will cover you with My hand while I pass by. Then I will take away My hand, and you shall see My back; but My face shall not be seen."
Exodus 33:21-23

Why didn't God show His face? Because the glory would be too great to handle for Moses. But even looking at His back, Moses returned from the mount, with his face shining so bright, that the people who saw it became afraid. Why did that happen? When the glory of God comes near, it immediately emphasizes our carnal human condition. Every part of us that is still in darkness, whether it is knowingly or unknowingly, is exposed by the bright Light of God. We know that God doesn't want to condemn us, but the realization of our own shortcomings, failures and sins can be pretty devastating when we become fully aware of it. Examples of this can be seen at the places where real revivals broke out. The first visible sign always was that people became aware of their carnal condition and started to cry out and shout out to God for forgiveness. This is what happened in The Netherlands as well, 250 years ago. And it will happen again.

In the old times, people always Anointed their whole face. They Anointed every part of skin that was exposed to the light, just like God covered every part of Moses, that was exposed to His glory. When the hand of God, that is covering His glory, is lifted, or partially lifted, it has an immediate effect and causes His glory to be released. The image of 'to draw the hand over', while anointing, represents the hand of God. After the face is Anointed, the hand is removed from the face and the face becomes exposed to the light again. The prophetic image of this is the hand of God being lifted, exposing us to His glory and light.

ANOINTING BY SPRINKLING

This way of Anointing is to sprinkle. This was not a common daily use, but for special occasions. When it comes to sprinkling, the Bible mentions three types of sprinkling:

- With the blood of sacrifice
- With water of purification
- With Anointing Oil

The blood of the sacrifice for forgiveness, the water of purification to cleanse and purify and the Anointing Oil for restoration or establishment of holiness and glory, by the power of the Holy Spirit in us. This is why people in some circles, still use the prophetic deed of sprinkling with wine (as the image of the Blood of Jesus), sprinkling with water and sprinkling with Anointing Oil. This is an image of returning to God, returning to holiness and returning to His presence, according the order of entering the Tabernacle. The first item you faced was the altar of sacrifice, the second was the brazen laver and after that you entered the Holy Place, where every item was Anointed with Anointing Oil, where the Golden Lampstand burned on fragrant oil, where the Altar of Incense burned on a mix with oil and where the Holy Anointing Oil was present as well.

The sprinkling of the blood is the most used form of sprinkling in the Bible. It is spoken of as the blood of the covenant (Exodus 24:8) and it was used to sprinkle the altar (Exodus 24:6), to sprinkle the priests and their garments (Exodus 29:21), to sprinkle the people as a confirmation of the covenant (Exodus 24:8), to sprinkle the ground before the entrance of the Holy Place (Leviticus 4:6), to sprinkle the people as the first step of cleansing and purification (Leviticus 14:6-7), to sprinkle a house that needed to be cleansed (Leviticus 14:51), to sprinkle the hands (2 Chronicles 35:11) and to sprinkle the mercy seat and the ground before it (Leviticus 16:14-15). So it speaks of the cleansing of the sin of people, garments, houses and places, before offering the blood at the mercy seat.

But Christ came as High Priest of the good things to come, with the greater and more perfect tabernacle not made with hands, that is, not of this creation. Not with the blood of goats and calves, but with His own blood He entered the Most Holy Place once for all, having obtained eternal redemption. For if the blood of bulls and goats and the ashes of a heifer, sprinkling the unclean, sanctifies for the purifying of the flesh, how much more shall the blood of Christ, who through the eternal Spirit offered Himself without spot to God, cleanse your conscience from dead works to serve the living God? And for this reason He is the Mediator of the new covenant, by means of death, for the redemption of the transgressions under the first covenant, that those who are called may receive the promise of the eternal inheritance.
Hebrews 9:11-15

Behold, My Servant shall deal prudently; He shall be exalted and extolled and be very high. Just as many were astonished at you, so His visage was marred more than any man, and His form more than the sons of men; So shall He sprinkle many nations. Kings shall shut their mouths at Him; for what had not been told them they shall see, and what they had not heard they shall consider.
Isaiah 52:13-15

Therefore, brethren, having boldness to enter the Holiest by the blood of Jesus, by a new and living way which He consecrated for us, through the veil, that is, His flesh, and having a High Priest over the house of God, let us draw near with a true heart in full assurance of faith, having our hearts sprinkled from an evil conscience and our bodies washed with pure water.
Hebrews 10:19-22

It still is amazing that, while the blood of the sacrifices in the Tabernacle and the Temple could only cleanse one from the outside, the Blood of Jesus is able to sprinkle our hearts, dealing with the cause of our problem. Everything and everyone where His blood is applied to, becomes free of sin. No matter how you look at it, that is huge!

And according to the law almost all things are purified with blood, and without shedding of blood there is no remission.
Hebrews 9:22

The next thing you came across, was the brazen laver, with the water of purification. This was the place where the priests had to wash and purify themselves, before entering the presence of the Lord. Before anyone was allowed to minister, no matter in what way, they needed to be cleansed of all uncleanness. Everyone who committed sin was considered unclean. But whenever someone touched something unclean, for example entering a place where sinful acts were committed or touching an item that was used to commit sin, they became unclean because of touching it. The pureness and holiness of the Lord is so far reaching, that He is the definition of pureness and holiness. Entering into His presence, without purifying yourself, would cause your immediate death.

So they shall wash their hands and their feet, lest they die. And it shall be a statute forever to them—to him and his descendants throughout their generations.
Exodus 30:21

Every smallest part of uncleanness is unable to face the glory of the Lord, without disastrous consequences. When the priests were appointed, they were ceremonially cleansed. This was done by sprinkling the water of purification on them (Numbers 8:7). But the people also needed to be cleansed, whenever they became unclean, by sprinkling the water of purification over them (Numbers 19:13). Every person who did not cleanse himself was to be cut off, was no longer a part of Israel and remained unclean for the rest of his life.

By the mouth of the prophet Ezekiel, God made a remarkable promise, in reference to the water of purification.

Then I will sprinkle clean water on you, and you shall be clean; I will cleanse you from all your filthiness and from all your idols. I will give you a new heart and put a new spirit within you; I will take the heart of stone out of your flesh and give you a heart of flesh. I will put My Spirit within you and cause you to walk in My statutes, and you will keep My judgments and do them.
Ezekiel 36:25-27

First God promises to cleanse, then He promises to give a new heart, then to give a new spirit, and then to put His Spirit in us. So first our life and our body is cleansed, but our heart and spirit are not cleansed, they are replaced by a new heart and a new spirit. As we know from the Old Testament, it was the sprinkling of the water that purified and cleansed. In these days, the sprinkling of water that cleanses us, is the Word that Jesus Christ spoke. It is the Word of Jesus Christ that cleanses us. Notice that Hebrews 10:22 tells us that our hearts are sprinkled with the Blood of Jesus, but that our bodies are cleansed with the pure water. It is the Blood of Jesus Christ that deals with the cause of our sin, the human heart, while the water of purification, which is the Word that Jesus has spoken, cleanses our body from sin. That means that all the negative results of sin can be broken, because of His forgiveness, because of His Blood, sprinkled on our hearts, because of the water of purification, the Word of Jesus Christ, sprinkled on our lives.

You are already clean because of the word which I have spoken to you. Abide in Me, and I in you. As the branch cannot bear fruit of itself, unless it abides in the vine, neither can you, unless you abide in Me. "I am the vine, you are the branches. He who abides in Me, and I in him, bears much fruit; for without Me you can do nothing.
John 15:3-5

This is why it is so incredibly important to stay in His Word, to read His Word, to meditate on His Word, to align our thoughts with His Word, to speak His Word. It is like a spiritual shower, cleansing us, over and over again. Wherever and whenever we need it. The more of His Word is in us, the more it will change us. Nothing else has that power. It is the Word that started everything. Because of the Word, this world came into being. You came into being, because of the Word. But the promise is even greater than that. Not only will the Word cleanse us, it will live in us, it will saturate every part of our being. After we are sprinkled and cleansed by the Word, the promise becomes even bigger.

On the last day, that great day of the feast, Jesus stood and cried out, saying, "If anyone thirsts, let him come to Me and drink. He who believes in Me, as the Scripture has said, out of his heart will flow rivers of living water." But this He spoke concerning the Spirit, whom those believing in Him would receive; for the Holy Spirit was not yet given, because Jesus was not yet glorified.
John 7:37-39

Here Jesus says that whoever believes in Him will receive the Holy Spirit, as the Scripture has said. That means that the Source of the Word will live in each and every one who believes in Jesus Christ. That is amazing! That means that the Word will not only cleanse us, it will also change us! It is the Spirit of the Anointed and the Anointing in us.

Finally there is the Anointing by sprinkling Anointing Oil. As we know, the Holy Spirit is in us, but the Anointing by sprinkling is the image of the Holy Spirit on us. That is not instead, but on top of His presence in us. After the forgiveness of sin and the cleansing of all uncleanness, this is the image of the restoration or establishment of His holiness and glory upon our lives, by the power of the Holy Spirit. This can be considered as a spiritual garment. He shall be with us, surrounding us by His glory, and He shall be in us.

The sprinkling of Anointing Oil is used to hallow people, items and places. The aim of this type of Anointing was not to appoint, but to hallow. This way of Anointing can be used to Anoint people, garments, items and places (like a Church building, a house etc.). An example of this can be seen in Exodus.

And you shall take some of the blood that is on the altar, and some of the anointing oil, and sprinkle it on Aaron and on his garments, on his sons and on the garments of his sons with him; and he and his garments shall

be hallowed, and his sons and his sons' garments with him.
Exodus 29:21

Take note that this prophetic action was not to appoint the priests. The Word says that it was meant to hallow them. The actual Anointing for appointment had already taken place when this type of Anointing was done.

ANOINTING BY POURING

The Anointing by pouring was and is only used to appoint people for ministry. Throughout the Old Testament, this type of Anointing was only used to appoint prophets, kings and priests. When they were Anointed for duty, the Holy Spirit would come over them and empower them. The Bible mentions several of these Anointings. But although one was Anointed by way of pouring, they were only referred to as the Lord's Anointed, when the Anointing was done, commissioned by God. Let's take a look at a few examples of Anointing by pouring.

And you shall take the anointing oil, pour it on his head, and anoint him.
Exodus 29:7

Then Samuel took a flask of oil and poured it on his head, and kissed him and said: "Is it not because the Lord has anointed you commander over His inheritance?
1 Samuel 1:10

Then Samuel took the horn of oil and anointed him in the midst of his brothers; and the Spirit of the Lord came upon David from that day forward. So Samuel arose and went to Ramah.
1 Samuel 16:13

Then Zadok the priest took a horn of oil from the tabernacle and anointed Solomon. And they blew the horn, and all the people said, "Long live King Solomon!"
1 Kings 1:39

Then the Lord said to him: "Go, return on your way to the Wilderness of

Damascus; and when you arrive, anoint Hazael as king over Syria. Also you shall anoint Jehu the son of Nimshi as king over Israel. And Elisha the son of Shaphat of Abel Meholah you shall anoint as prophet in your place.
1 Kings 19:15-16

Although I couldn't find how prophets were Anointed exactly, except that it was through pouring, I could find that kings were Anointed by pouring in the form of a crown. That is pouring a circle on the top of the head, in the form of a crown. Priests were Anointed by pouring in the form of an X. This happened from the back of the head, sideward to the eyebrows, from left to right and from right to left.

ANOINTING WITH THE FLASK OR WITH THE HORN
The difference between Anointing with a flask or with the horn was only mentioned with Anointing by pouring. In other words, only with the Anointing and appointment of leaders. The horn was a reference to the horns of the Altar of Incense. The Tabernacle (and later the Temple) had two altars with horns. The first was the Altar of Sacrifice or Brazen Altar, which stood in the courtyard. The second altar was the Altar of Incense, which stood in the Holy Place. The horns represented the divine Truth of God, the mercy of God and strength of God.

I will love You, O Lord, my strength. The Lord is my rock and my fortress and my deliverer; My God, my strength, in whom I will trust; My shield and the horn of my salvation, my stronghold.
Psalm 18:1-2

In the old days, when someone was about to be condemned, he could grab the horns of the altar for mercy. When his intentions were good, meaning that he didn't commit his sin intentionally, his life would be spared (Exodus 21:14). The horn of Anointing refers to the horns of the Altar of Incense. This altar was not to be touched by the blood of sacrifice. The blood of sacrifice was only to be applied to the horns of the Altar of Incense, while the rest of the altar needed to be free of blood. This altar represented prayer and intercession, or relationship with God. As you may have guessed by now, the horns of the altar referred to our Messiah, Jesus Christ. He Who revealed Himself as the Way, the Truth and the Life. He Who became our Horn of Salvation.

There I will make the horn of David grow; I will prepare a lamp for My Anointed. His enemies I will clothe with shame, but upon Himself His crown shall flourish.
Psalm 132:17-18

Blessed is the Lord God of Israel, for He has visited and redeemed His people, and has raised up a horn of salvation for us in the house of His servant David.
Luke 1:68-69

All the kings that were not a part of the family line of Jesus, were Anointed by pouring from the flask. All the kings that were part of the family line of Jesus, were Anointed by pouring from the Horn. Although it may seem that the difference between Anointing with the flask or with the Horn is whether one was anointed on the initiative of man or on the initiative of God, that is not the case here. King Jehu, who was Anointed for the task to cut off the house of Ahab (and Jezebel), was Anointed on the Lord's initiative, although he was Anointed by pouring from a flask (2 Kings 9:1-13). The Anointing from the Horn has everything to do with the family line of Jesus Christ, the Son of the Living God.

The Anointing from the Horn is something that is not used anymore in these days, for Jesus Christ is the only Horn of Salvation, from Whom our spiritual Anointing flows and is poured upon us. We are the sons of oil, shining bright from the Anointing that He has poured over us. The Anointing of Salvation and the Royal Priesthood, with Jesus Christ as our High Priest in Heaven.

CHAPTER 8

WHO, WHAT AND WHEN TO ANOINT

When it comes to Anointing people and things, the question always arises when can we Anoint and who is allowed to Anoint in what circumstance. In order to explain all of this, it is important to understand the God given authority structures. Most authority is not initiated by God, but since God respects our choices, He does appoint all authority. As a result, He commands us to be subject to the governing authorities.

Let every soul be subject to the governing authorities. For there is no authority except from God, and the authorities that exist are appointed by God.
Romans 13:1

It is very important to understand that God will never bypass His authority structure! We are to submit to each and every form of authority, as long as it is in line with the Word of God. That means we have to obey our government, and all the laws, and that we have to obey our spiritual leaders.

When the laws of our government tell us to do things that are against the Word of God, and that would make us commit sin, we are to ignore those rules and to follow the highest authority, which is God. An example of this would be when our government would command us to bow before other gods, to commit murder, to lie etc. In some nations, the government forbids people to follow Christ, to mention His name, to own a Bible, to pray to Jesus, to gather in His name etc. These things are going against the Word of God, and we are to obey the Word of God above everything else. The Holy Spirit will help us to do so, for it is impossible to do this from our own strength or efforts. But other than that, we are to follow and obey all the laws the government gives us. We are to be the example of God's righteousness in our nation, lovers of righteousness and justice.

Why am I telling this? The Anointing for personal use is always allowed. You do not need permission for that. But when it comes to Anointing others or to anointing things or places, God's authority structure always applies. God is the One Who appointed each and every position. If we want to receive His blessing, if we want to do anything more than just a religious act, and if we want it to have any spiritual effect, we have to follow His authority structure. We can only receive blessing from those whose authority we acknowledge. For example, David was Anointed as king, by order of God Himself, but at that point he was not yet acknowledged as one by the people. The real change for Israel came after they acknowledged him as well. First the people of Judah Anointed David as their king (2 Samuel 2:4). This happened after he was already Anointed by the prophet. Later the people of Israel Anointed him as king as well (2 Samuel 5:3). Only from that moment could he be a blessing to Israel and only from that moment could they receive the blessing through God's Anointed. These universal spiritual principles still apply today. Now what does God's authority structure look like?

GOD'S AUTHORITY STRUCTURE IN GENERAL
Father God -> King Jesus Christ -> The Ecclesia -> The earthly government -> The people

GOD'S AUTHORITY STRUCTURE IN THE ECCLESIA
Father God -> King Jesus Christ -> Apostles -> Prophets -> Teachers -> Evangelists -> Pastors -> Husbands -> Wives -> Children

Let me clear this up, before there is any misunderstanding. In the natural we are to submit to the government, since God has appointed all the authority over us. However, in the spirit, the Ecclesia (the governing body of Christ a.k.a. the Church) has the highest authority in a nation. Our battle is not against governments, not against earthly authorities, but against spiritual authorities.

For we do not wrestle against flesh and blood, but against principalities, against powers, against the rulers of the darkness of this age, against spiritual hosts of wickedness in the heavenly places.
Ephesians 6:12

Where are these of ours? In the heavenly places. So we honor and respect the appointed authority over us, but we wrestle against the powers and the rulers of the darkness of this eon, the spiritual hosts of wickedness in the heavenly places.

Jesus Christ gave us the example of divine leadership. He reigned by serving. He never dominated, never used manipulation or intimidation, but He served. He washed the feet of His disciples. He knew how to distinguish man's behavior from the spiritual powers behind it. So in the natural He served, while in the spiritual realm, He reigned and crushed each and every opposition. In the natural He seemed like a weak Person. After all, at first glance, it doesn't seem very powerful to be tortured and to hang on a cross, helpless and alone. Yet that was the most powerful act. The ultimate act of serving was to lay down His life for us. Jesus Christ willingly and knowingly submitted to the authority of His Father, as He requires us to submit to the authority He appointed over us.

ANOINTING OF LEADERS
When it comes to Anointing someone to appoint him or her in a position, we always have to keep the following in mind. A private cannot promote someone to sergeant, just like a sergeant cannot promote anyone to be a general. A private can promote no one, because he has the lowest rank and needs to learn and grow first. He needs to become ready for battle, before he deserves any promotion. A sergeant can promote anyone lower in rank, but only to the rank he/she has. So a person can only be promoted by someone who is of a higher rank. Like one of my friends always says: "You cannot buy a police uniform and be a police officer from that moment on. You have to be appointed by the Police Commissioner."

As Christians, we are supposed to be led by the Holy Spirit. We are supposed to willingly and knowingly submit to His authority and His will. That means that He makes the decisions for us and that we listen and comply. All authority is appointed by God, but if we want someone who is chosen by God, who is appointed by God's initiative, and thus become the Lord's Anointed, then we should listen to the Holy Spirit. Even if that means that we need to Anoint the least likely person as leader over us.

Remember, God has a thing with the least likely persons. David was the least likely person, when the prophet Samuel came. Yet God choose him to be king over His people. And look at the incredible history. Even Jesus Christ is referred to as the son of David! Imagine what God can do in your Church or in your life, through the least likely persons.

In the case of Anointing and appointing a leader, we ask the Holy Spirit for the right person. We clear our minds from our thoughts and ideas, and start listening to what He has to say. Then we compare it with the others who did the same. Like each body has two ears, the body of Christ has more than one ear as well. So if the others hear the same, it can be considered as 'tested'. Then we can Anoint the person who was pointed out by the Holy Spirit. If there is someone of a higher rank around, then they can Anoint and appoint this person in their God given rank. If not, but if the Holy Spirit has clearly has spoken, the person can be Anointed on behalf of the authority of the Holy Spirit Himself. Sometimes God also sends one of His Anointed leaders with the specific task to Anoint and appoint someone. Either way, His will shall be done.

What happens if we Anoint and appoint someone, without consulting the Holy Spirit and based on our own feelings and insights? Then we get an 'Absolom' authority. An authority that was initiated by man, not by God. Absolom was anointed as king over Israel, by the people of Israel (2 Samuel 19:10). So his authority over Israel was real. Yet he was never addressed as 'the Lord's Anointed' by God. Each and every act, based upon our own knowledge, wisdom and understanding, without consulting God, is considered as an act of rebellion against God. Remember that satan seduced Adam and Eve to trust on knowledge as well. That is how mankind fell into sin.

ANOINTING FOR PERSONAL USE
I've already said it, but I can't emphasize it enough. The Anointing for personal use is always allowed. You don't need any permission from any leader in order to use it. Jesus Himself instructed us to use it. All the people in the Old Testament used it. All the people in the New Testament used it. Even the early Church, until the ninth century, used it. If you haven't read the chapter "Who Is Allowed To Use Anointing Oil?" yet, I

advise you to do so. It contains all the answers in regard to the personal use of Anointing Oil.

ANOINTING THE SICK

The Anointing of the sick is the most known Anointing that people know nowadays. This Anointing doesn't come instead of the personal use of Anointing Oil, but on top of it. However, it is done in the same way as personal Anointing, which is by Mashah (to smear, to draw the hand over the face). The Word of God gives a specific instruction for the Anointing of the sick. In this case we are to call the elders of the Ecclesia (the Church) and to let them pray over and Anoint the sick person. In other words, we're talking about those who are supposed to be mature in their faith. Mature in knowledge, mature in understanding, mature in insight, mature in wisdom and mature in moving and acting in faith.

Is anyone among you sick? Let him call for the elders of the church, and let them pray over him, anointing him with oil in the name of the Lord. And the prayer of faith will save the sick, and the Lord will raise him up. And if he has committed sins, he will be forgiven.
James 5:14-15

During the process of praying for the sick, there have been so many mistakes. The biggest mistake of all is that the faith of the sick person should be of any value, in order to receive the healing. I can't emphasize it enough that that is not true and it is not what the Word of God says. It is the prayer of faith that will heal him. That means that the faith of the persons, in this case the elders of the Ecclesia, is of value. If they lack faith, nothing will happen. That cannot and may not be blamed on the sick person. The elders are supposed to be mature in moving and acting in faith. If you are an elder and if you know you are lacking faith, there is only one way to get it. Find everything that the Word of God has to say about healing and step out in faith. Just start doing it (Mark 6:13). When nothing happens, keep on stepping out in faith and refuse to believe anything other than the Word of God. Your faith will be tested, but if you persevere in faith, you will see it happen eventually or immediately. As for the faith of the sick person, once he is healed, it takes faith in order to stay healed. Stand on the promises of God. Once you have seen what the power of Jesus has done, by healing your body or by healing your emotional wounds, hold on to that faith by holding on to the Word of God. Expose every lie by confronting each and every lie in your thoughts with the Truth from the Word of God.

Last but not least, we also have to deal with the way people pray for the sick. There are many people, leaders included, who ask God or Jesus to lay His hands on the sick or who ask God if He wants to heal the sick person. And none of these prayers are ever answered. Let me tell you why by answering both questions.

Is Jesus willing to lay His hands on the sick person? No. He will not come down from heaven to lay His hands on a sick person. What was the commission He gave us? That He would come down to do it for us?

They will lay hands on the sick, and they will recover.
Mark 16:18

I don't see "I will lay My hands on the sick" anywhere in the Word of God. Who is Jesus talking about when He said "They"? He talked about "Those who believe". That is you. That are all your brothers and sisters who are in Christ. You are purchased by the blood of Jesus Christ, the Son of the Living God. Your body, soul and spirit belong to Him. So when you lay your hands on the sick, those are the hands of Jesus. Furthermore He has given you authority!

Behold, I give you the authority to trample on serpents and scorpions, and over all the power of the enemy, and nothing shall by any means hurt you.
Luke 10:19

So you are purchased by the blood of Jesus Christ, because of which Jesus Christ now has ownership over your body and your hands, the hands you are supposed to lay on the sick. You are clothed with the authority of Jesus Christ Himself. To do what? To stand by and to ask Him to do it? Then why did He give you the commission and the authority? Indeed! He gave it to you to do something with it. To be His representative on earth. To do the same works He did. That is including healing the sick.

Does God want to heal the sick person? Of course He wants that!

But He was wounded for our transgressions, He was bruised for our iniquities; the chastisement for our peace was upon Him, and by His stripes we are healed.
Isaiah 53:5

This verse doesn't say that we will be healed, it says we are healed. It is already done in the spiritual realm. That tells us everything about His will and desire to heal His people. The only thing we have to do is to apply that healing that He has already purchased for us. How did Jesus heal the sick? He commanded the sickness to go out and He proclaimed: "Be healed!". That's how He did it, that's how we are supposed to do it, in His name, by His authority.

ANOINTING FOR A SPECIFIC TASK
Sometimes God gives a person a specific task. The Anointing can (and is) also be applied to these situations. That means that God gives you the authority and power you need for that specific situation and task. The Anointing is – once again – the empowerment by the Holy Spirit. If He commands us to do something, we go in His authority and by His strength. If we act upon our own will, we also go in our own authority and our own strength. That is not the smartest thing to do. God wants us to wait for Him, and when He says "Go!", that's when we step out. An example of this is Jehu, who was Anointed to cut off the house of Ahab (the husband of Jezebel).

Jehu the son of Nimshi, whom the Lord had anointed to cut off the house of Ahab.
2 Chronicles 22:7b

As always, we have to be dependent on the Holy Spirit. As for the when or how to Anoint someone for a specific task, I can only say to follow the lead of the Holy Spirit. Each situation is different and He knows best what to do.

ANOINTING FOR DELIVERANCE

There is a spiritual world around us that is very real and very present. Just like God and His angels are moving in the spiritual realm, so does the satan and the evil spirits. These evil spirits cannot bind us, unless there is sin in our life. When we commit sin, that opens the door for evil spirits to make us a slave of sin. The ministry of deliverance is basically to get rid of the sin and to cast the demons out. We are called to do the works of Jesus Christ, and this was one of His works on earth. Like He said, those who believe will cast out demons (Mark 16:17). A Christian cannot be possessed by demons, because possession suggests ownership. As Christians, Jesus has the ownership over us. But we can be demonized, meaning that demons can keep us a prisoner to sin. From the Word of God we know that these demons are using our bodies to commit those sins. But Jesus Christ has provided a solution for that as well, by giving us authority over every power of the enemy (Luke 10:19).

As we have seen in the previous chapters, the Anointing stands for purification, hallowing and restoration. That means erasing every legal ground that our enemy had in our lives. The sins are confessed and forgiven, holiness is restored. From that moment no evil power has the right to remain in our lives and can be expelled. During the prayer of deliverance, the Anointing with Anointing Oil has a huge and immediate effect. The whole spiritual realm is very aware of the meaning of the prophetic deed of faith of Anointing a person. The Light of God is then released and the enemy is exposed. Again, when and how to Anoint is something you will have to do upon instruction of the Holy Spirit. He will guide you and He will tell you what to do, or what fragrance to use. For example, in the natural world, snakes hate the fragrance of frankincense & myrrh. In the spiritual realm that is no different.

ANOINTING ITEMS AND GARMENTS

When you want to entrust and dedicate an item or a garment to the Lord, you can do so by sprinkling Anointing Oil on it, in the name of Jesus Christ. The sprinkling of Anointing Oil is used to hallow people, items and places. The aim of this type of Anointing was not to appoint, but to hallow. The items and garments that were Anointed, were to be considered holy from that moment on. Keep in mind that every item in the Tabernacle, every item in the Temple and every item in the Kingdom of Heaven is Anointed, just as God is Anointed. This is a prophetic deed of faith, like every other Anointing.

ANOINTING PLACES

The same principles used with the Anointing of items apply here as well. I'll give you an example. Whenever we enter a new house, apartment or a new Church building, we don't know what kind of sins were committed there. Evil powers are not only 'using' people, but also items and places that were used to commit sin. That makes that item or place unholy. When we signed the contract of our home, our home became our responsibility. We have to live in it and we have the authority over it. So we kneeled down in our home and stood in the gap on behalf of all the people that lived here before us, and we asked God for forgiveness for each and every sin that had taken place on these grounds. Then we've Anointed the house, hallowing it in the name of Jesus Christ, by sprinkling Anointing Oil in each and every room and by Anointing the doorposts. As the priest of this home and this family, I have made Jesus Christ the highest authority in this place. In my home, it is Jesus Christ Who reigns, and I wanted to show that to the whole spiritual realm, by Anointing and dedicating this place to Him. The same was done in the Tabernacle, the Temple and in many other places that needed hallowing.

ANOINTING OF HONORABLE GUESTS

The anointing of honorable guests is a custom that is not used very often anymore. But it has a significant meaning in the spiritual realm. First of all, to Anoint an honorable person and guest is to respect that person. I know, that probably doesn't mean much, because in these days and in our society, the word 'respect' has become something shady. For most of the people living in these days, the word 'respect' has a political load. It is often used for political correctness, but the original meaning is something entirely different. To have respect means to have regard, esteem and appreciation for a person, because of his qualities, achievements and skills. It is a form of honor. For this reason it is very dangerous to have and show respect to other religions, to other gods, for it is a form of idolatry.

Besides respect, the Anointing of an honorable guest also means to recognize him as such. When Jesus walked on earth, many people acknowledged Him as a remarkable person, some even as a prophet, but never as the Messiah and Son of God. The lack of giving respect and recognition to Jesus, can be seen in Luke 7. One of the Pharisees had invited Him to eat with him, but he had not treated Jesus as an honorable guest, which was an insult at that time. It was a sign that he considered himself to be more honorable than Jesus. But then a sinful woman came into the house and Anointed Jesus, giving Him the respect, honor and recognition He deserves.

Then He turned to the woman and said to Simon, "Do you see this woman? I entered your house; you gave Me no water for My feet, but she has washed My feet with her tears and wiped them with the hair of her head. You gave Me no kiss, but this woman has not ceased to kiss My feet since the time I came in. You did not anoint My head with oil, but this woman has anointed My feet with fragrant oil. Therefore I say to you, her sins, which are many, are forgiven, for she loved much. But to whom little is forgiven, the same loves little." Then He said to her, "Your sins are forgiven."
Luke 7:44-48

The Anointing of an honorable guest was and is the respect and recognition of that person as such. God can and will only bless us if we accept, respect and recognize the people He has send to bless us. Not because of these people, but because of the One Who appointed and Anointed them. So we don't worship people, but we show God our appreciation and respect, by accepting the person He has send to bless us. If we reject a person who was send by God, we reject His blessing as well. It was in this light that Jesus said the following.

For I say to you, you shall see Me no more till you say, 'Blessed is He who comes in the name of the Lord!'
Matthew 23:39

Jesus will only show Himself at the moment He is recognized and respected as the Messiah, the Son of the Living God. Likewise, His Anointing will only flow when we accept the ones who were send to us by Him and in His name. This acceptance, respect and recognition was and is shown by Anointing that person in the name of our Messiah, Jesus Christ.

CHAPTER 9

THE WAY TO SPIRITUAL ANOINTING

Anointing Oil is not a miracle cure or a miracle drug. It's not something magic. It is just pure olive oil with a fragrance. It only starts to become valuable, when it is used in faith, as a prophetic deed. It is not the oil that causes God's power to be released, it is our faith in Him that does that. A prophetic deed is basically an act you do in the natural world, to make your faith visible. It is also an act of obedience. The Anointing with Anointing Oil is an image of the empowerment with the Holy Spirit and of the Spiritual Anointing. It is the image of the glory of God with us, an image of God with us.

We are living in a world which can be seen, heard, smelled, tasted and touched. Our senses enable us to be aware of the world around us. As we all know, we can only act based upon that of which we are aware of. Because of this reason, we are aware of the world around us and we know that it's real. But the Bible is teaching us that this world is not the only thing that is real. There is another world among us. A spiritual world, that which cannot naturally be seen, heard, smelled, tasted or touched. But it is very real and it is among us. That spiritual world runs parallel to our natural world. The apostle Paul emphasized the existence of this world in his letter to the Ephesians.

For we do not wrestle against flesh and blood, but against principalities, against powers, against the rulers of the darkness of this age, against spiritual hosts of wickedness in the heavenly places.
Ephesians 6:12

So we do wrestle, we do battle, against persons we cannot perceive with our senses. But they are real. Very real. It shows us that there is something around us, another world. This is the spiritual world, or the spiritual realm, where God, all his angels and our enemy is moving in.

Some receive the ability to sense it with one or more of their senses, as a part of their Anointing and ministry. But even if you can't sense it, it still is real. In this world there is an Anointing as well. Some think that the actions we take in the natural world establish something in the spiritual world. But in fact, it is the other way around. Our natural world and everything we can perceive with our senses, is a result of what was first established in the spiritual world and then became a reality in our natural world. Sometimes the result in the spiritual realm immediately becomes a reality in our natural world, while at other times it takes some time before any result can be perceived, while it is indeed established in the spiritual realm.

When we Anoint in the natural world, we do not do that in order to establish something in the spiritual realm. We do it to show our faith in what is already established in the spiritual realm. And because of that faith, the results will immediately or eventually be perceived in our natural world. An example of this is the healing of the sick. Healing was and is already established in the spiritual realm, by our Lord Jesus Christ. The Word of God clearly says that we are healed by His stripes (Isaiah 53:5). It does not speak of "will be healed" but of "are healed". It is already done. The faith of the one(s) who pray for the sick and the anointing of the sick, are a prophetic act of faith in that established reality. When Jesus cried out "It is finished!", that included sickness. And so much more.

At other times things do need to be established in the spiritual realm. But that doesn't happen by establishing them in the natural world. There are strongholds of the enemy, there are principalities, powers, rulers of the darkness of this eon and spiritual hosts of wickedness among the celestial ones in the spiritual realm. There is a battle going on and its cause is in the spiritual realm. Everything we see in the natural world is a result of what already happened in the spiritual realm. If we want to make any change in a situation, we need to start there. The weapons we have are the proclaimed Word of God and prayer. When do these weapons become effective? Whenever they are used from a heart that has no doubt.

For assuredly, I say to you, whoever says to this mountain, 'Be removed

and be cast into the sea,' and does not doubt in his heart, but believes that
those things he says will be done, he will have whatever he says. Therefore I
say to you, whatever things you ask when you pray, believe that you receive
them, and you will have them.
Mark 11:23-24

Whenever we ask something, we need to have a heart without doubt. But how do we get rid of doubt? That question can as easily be answered as "How do we get rid of darkness?". We do not get rid of the darkness by expelling it, but by simply turning on the light. Likewise, we do not get rid of doubt by expelling it, but by building faith. Romans 10:17 tells us that faith comes by hearing, and hearing by the Word of God. So whenever we speak the Word of God, we are building faith. It's a collaboration between you and God. Whenever you start to speak His Word, He will add faith to you. So whenever we ask something from God, whenever we establish something in that spiritual realm, we have to believe that His Word is true and that we have obtained that which we asked for. From that moment on we are adjusting our actions to that faith. Even if the results cannot be immediately perceived. We have to trust Jesus, that He is faithful to His Word and that it is established in the spiritual realm.

As there is an Anointing in the natural world, likewise there is a spiritual Anointing as well. While the Anointing used to be something that was exclusively for prophets, kings and priests, we now all have been called for a Royal priesthood. At the moment that we've accepted Jesus Christ as our Messiah and Savior, He became our High Priest in heaven and we became His bride. Not only were we saved, we were and are called as well. Not for our own benefit, but for a world in need. You have received an Anointing.

Now He who establishes us with you in Christ and has anointed us is God,
who also has sealed us and given us the Spirit in our hearts as a guarantee.
2 Corinthians 1:21-22

But you have an anointing from the Holy One, and you know all things.
1 John 2:20

How God anointed Jesus of Nazareth with the Holy Spirit and with power, who went about doing good and healing all who were oppressed by the devil, for God was with Him.
Acts 10:38

Through these Bible verses we can see the clear connection between the Anointing and the Holy Spirit. You are Anointed in the spiritual realm and the perceivable result of that is that the Holy Spirit dwells in you. You are Anointed in God, you are sealed with the Holy Spirit as a guarantee. Because of this Anointing in God, and the gift of the Holy Spirit in you, you now have access to all His knowledge, wisdom and understanding. That is the opposite of Hosea 4:6, where God says that His people are being destroyed because of a lack of knowledge. For this reason, the prophet Isaiah made the following statement, on behalf of God.

And the yoke will be destroyed because of the anointing oil.
Isaiah 10:27

Basically we have two options. We can choose not to be led by the Holy Spirit and to try to justify ourselves through the law, which will lead us to destruction. Or we can choose to be led by the Holy Spirit, to be free of the consequences of the law, to let the Holy Spirit write His laws in our heart and to move in the opposite direction of destruction. That is the moment when the yoke is destroyed. The original Hebrew text can also be translated as "the yoke will be destroyed because of the fat". When the Bible refers to "the fat", it very often points to the Anointing (Oil). In this case it means both. The yoke is placed on the neck of someone, as can be seen in the same verse. The Anointing will cause us to be filled with the fullness of God. That doesn't mean that it takes a lot of power to destroy the yoke. It means that our neck will grow so (spiritually) fat, that the yoke simply cannot restrain us anymore and breaks because the size of our neck has exceeded the size of the yoke. How does that happen? The more we are filled with His knowledge, wisdom and insight, the fatter we grow in the spirit. And in this case that is a good thing. It is a healthy fatness, for it is the fullness of God in us, through His Spirit, Who reveals all things to us.

Like I've mentioned before, the spiritual realm runs parallel to our natural and visible world. Yes, we are Anointed, but in the spiritual realm there are more Anointings than one, just as in our natural world. We are Anointed with the Anointing for salvation, restoration and access to God's knowledge, wisdom and understanding. But that does not yet make us fit for duty. It doesn't mean we're ready for service. In a way you could say that the Holy Spirit and the Anointing are leading you away from carnality, away from trusting on your own wisdom, knowledge and understanding. When people look at those who walk, talk and act in the Spirit, many get the feeling that they will never get there. They measure their lives with those people and come to the conclusion that they will never be able to reach the same. But they forget the most important thing. None of these people, who walk, talk and act in the Spirit, have achieved the slightest bit on their own strength, wisdom, knowledge or understanding. Not even one. None of them were able to use their own capabilities to reach that level. Not even one. Each and every person had to humble himself and had to come to the place of total dependency, the place where they had to surrender every last bit of their lives to God. In other words, it is all about losing control and surrendering all of that control to God. It goes without saying that none of these people were able to do that instantly. It is a process for everyone. It is a growth process. But in that process of growing in faith and in being depended on God, it is His power that transforms you. It is His power that turns you into everything you never thought was possible.

Now you have reached the part of this study that most people despise. Everyone wants the blessings. Everyone wants the Anointing. Everyone wants to move in the supernatural. But few are willing to pay the price that is attached to it. The way to all of this is a small way. It is a way that demands a lot of toll. There is a price to pay, but it cannot be bought with money or material possessions (2 Kings 5:26-27). The price we have to pay is that our lives are no longer about ourselves, about our desires, about our will and not about our emotions. I'm not saying we don't have all those things as a Christian, but I'm saying that they no longer should take the highest priority. Our 'flesh' needs to die (Romans 8:12-17). That means a shift of focus. It's no longer "What do I desire?", but "What does the Word of God desire?". It's no longer "What do I want?", but "What does the Word of God want?". It's no longer "What do I feel?", but "What does God feel?". We need to learn to align our desires, will and emotions with the Word of God. That's where our safety is.

Seek first the kingdom of God and His righteousness, and all these things shall be added to you.
Matthew 6:33

God is not indifferent to our desires, will or emotions. But they are a bad counselor for our lives. The worst decisions with the worst consequences are made from our own desires, will and emotions. It has nothing to do with God and has everything to do with our 'flesh'. Whenever all these things, our flesh, our carnal nature, are no longer in charge, that's when the change begins. That's when the spiritual Anointing starts to grow. At that moment you start to grow to becoming a useful instrument in the hand of God. The more we die to our 'self', the more room it will give to God in our lives. That is not an easy way or an easy process. At many times it will be painful. Your dreams, your emotions, your will and your desires may seem totally crushed at times. Maybe even for a very long time. In these times we are so used to instant results, that we totally forget that most people in the Bible had to wait for many years before they were able to see or perceive even the slightest bit of God's promises. Their dreams, emotions, will and desires were totally crushed for a long long time. But the outcome of the promise that followed was so much greater than their suffering.

We learn through trials, through hardships, through pain. That is how we are spiritually shaped. That is how we grow to spiritual maturity and to the increase of God's Anointing in our lives. The image of the oil is an example of that. All the potential, all the talents and even the Anointing are laid in your life by God. But the only way to get it out and to get the most pure form of it, is done in the exact same way how the oil is extracted. Just like the olives need to be crushed in order to get the oil from it, in the same way our 'flesh' needs to be crushed as well. Just like the freshly ground oil needs to be heated in order to cleanse it from all the dirt and to make it pure, in the same way we have to go through the fire as well. Just to be clear, that is not the same fire as the hell fire. The fire of God can be best described as the purifying and cleansing fire of His passion and love. Although it may be painful at the moment itself, it will turn you into everything God wants you to be.

In the very beginning of mankind, Adam and Eve traded their dependency on God for trust in knowledge, from a motivation of rebellion and pride. That action changed the course of every human being that would ever live on earth. Instead of trusting God and depending on His knowledge, wisdom and insight, they choose to do the opposite. Since that moment, every human being has the carnal desire to do the same. And we need to fight to muzzle that desire. We need to align ourselves with the Word of God. His thoughts need to be our thoughts. His will needs to be our will. His joy needs to be our joy. What He considers as sin, we need to consider as sin. What He considers as righteousness, we need to consider as righteousness. It is a change of heart and a change of thoughts.

Trust in the Lord with all your heart, and lean not on your own understanding; In all your ways acknowledge Him, and He shall direct your paths. Do not be wise in your own eyes; Fear the Lord and depart from evil. It will be health to your flesh, and strength to your bones.
Proverbs 3:5-8

We have learned about the existence of evil spirits and about the existence of curses. And many times we assume that that is going on, when things get tough in our lives. While that may be the case, we must also not forget that there is such a thing as trials and testing. There is not a single person who moves under and in the Anointing, who just received that instantly. They all had to go through hard times, through trials and testing, even until the point where they thought they could take no more. A season where everything you do seems to fail. Since almost nobody teaches about this anymore, many people get so discouraged, sad and depressed, that they want to give up, believing there is no hope left for them. I am telling you that this is a normal part of your Christian life. You haven't failed, but you're in the test. All of this is meant to prepare you for ministry, to align your thoughts, your heart and your character with the Word of God, in order to make you meek and low. It is the place where you die and where the life of Jesus takes over in you. That isn't easy and it takes faith to remain standing. Only those who stay in His Word, who hold fast to His promises, will overcome. Even if it takes years or even decades. We must come to the conclusion that God is and always will be faithful to His Word. Maybe you are in testing and trials right now. Maybe you have received all those great promises, but you haven't seen anything yet. Maybe you're in this season for years already, without any sign. I am telling you that it is a normal part of the Christian life. You haven't done anything wrong. God just considers you so valuable, that He choose you to prepare you for His service. Even if it means the salvation of one soul. He is preparing you for a task. And even when it feels like you can take no more, that is the moment to hold on. That is the moment to not be led by your feelings or emotions, but to hold on to the promises of God. Like the old song by Russel Carter says: "Standing on the promises that cannot fail, when the howling storms of doubt and fear assail, by the living Word of God I shall prevail, standing on the promises of God." Don't give up. You're not finished, you're far from finished. This is just the beginning and the best is yet to come! Hold fast! This too shall pass.

The poor and needy seek water, but there is none, their tongues fail for thirst. I, the Lord, will hear them; I, the God of Israel, will not forsake them. I will open rivers in desolate heights, and fountains in the midst of the valleys; I will make the wilderness a pool of water, and the dry land springs of water. I will plant in the wilderness the cedar and the acacia tree, the myrtle and the oil tree; I will set in the desert the cypress tree and the pine and the box tree together, that they may see and know, and consider and understand together, that the hand of the Lord has done this, and the Holy One of Israel has created it.
Isaiah 41:17-20

Though the fig tree may not blossom, nor fruit be on the vines; Though the labor of the olive may fail, and the fields yield no food; Though the flock may be cut off from the fold, and there be no herd in the stalls—Yet I will rejoice in the Lord, I will joy in the God of my salvation. The Lord God is my strength; He will make my feet like deer's feet, and He will make me walk on my high hills.
Habakkuk 3:17-19

CHAPTER 10

ACTING IN THE SPIRITUAL ANOINTING

Acting in the Spiritual Anointing means to be sensitive for when and how the Holy Spirit wants to move through you, and being available for that. Like we've seen in the previous chapter, it takes some time, preparation and lessons in order to learn that. It can easily be missed if we don't know what to look for. But when He has prepared us, through trials and testing, we become a usable instrument in His hands. That is the moment where we come out of that season of wilderness, of drought and of failure. It is the moment when we have learned to be humble, meek and dependent. This is why it is so important to consult God for whom to appoint as leaders. For we do not know who is ready yet. We haven't seen the trials and testing that people had to go through. We haven't seen how they responded to it and if their character is aligned with God's Word yet. All these things are not visible from the outside, for it lives in our hearts. Only God is the One Who searches our hearts and thoughts daily and Who is able to do so. The further we grow to higher spiritual levels, the lower and meeker we become in the natural world.

Whoever exalts himself will be humbled, and he who humbles himself will be exalted.
Matthew 23:12

For by strength no man shall prevail. The adversaries of the Lord shall be broken in pieces; From heaven He will thunder against them. The Lord will judge the ends of the earth. He will give strength to His king, and exalt the horn of His anointed.
1 Samuel 2:9-10

When the time of preparation, trials and testing is over, God will appoint and Anoint you for your mission, ministry or service. From that moment you are considered as one who acts according to God's heart and mind (1

Samuel 2:35). The Lord Himself will exalt you. He will openly reward you for your faithfulness and for not giving up. He will do so in the presence of your enemies (Psalm 23:5). When you love righteousness and hate wickedness, you will receive God's Anointing with the oil of gladness, just as Jesus received it for the exact same reason (Psalm 45:7). You will stand as an olive tree in the presence of our God (Psalm 52:8), rooted in His love (Ephesians 3:17). The Anointing will be the restoration of your authority and dignity (2 Chronicles 28:15, Ezekiel 16:9).

THE BIGGEST TEST OF ALL

Trials and tests will come and go in your life. Whether we're aware of it or not, God is testing us all the time. When you have come out of the testing and trials that were meant to make you ready for duty, there is one part that appears in every job description in the army of the Lord. That description will never change and will be used to measure your life with.

Will the Lord be pleased with thousands of rams, ten thousand rivers of oil? Shall I give my firstborn for my transgression, the fruit of my body for the sin of my soul? He has shown you, O man, what is good; and what does the Lord require of you but to do justly, to love mercy, and to walk humbly with your God?
Micah 6:7,8

The trials and tests will continue, but the trials and test will change. Every lesson has the aim to teach you something. A lesson will go on and on, until you've learned what God wanted you to learn. Then the next lesson will start. These lessons will help you to grow to higher spiritual levels and to discover all the authority you have, and how to use it for the Kingdom. I agree with all those people who say that we have received all the authority. That is Biblical, as can be seen in Luke 10:19. But what good is authority when you don't know the measure of it, when you don't know how far it goes and when you don't know when or how to use it? So yes, you have the authority, but we all need to learn how to walk in it. The lessons are meant to do that. Truth and knowledge can only be used if we know it and if we're aware of it. The same applies for authority. The more you learn in those lessons, the more you will be able to use the authority God gave you.

How do I know that you can get out of that season of trials and testing? First of all because God is faithful. Secondly, because God is not out to make your life miserable. And thirdly, because all the trials and testing are working to make you ready for the biggest test of all. That is a test where the majority unfortunately fails. That test is called "success".

Whenever we're in pain, we're constantly aware of it. It's always there, reminding us that something is wrong and in need of healing. Whether that's physical or emotional. It will not go away until the issue is dealt with. But the remarkable thing is that the exact opposite applies for the lack of pain. Whenever we're doing well, and when we don't have any pain, we're not aware at all. You are aware now, because I'm telling you this, but you're not walking around, being constantly reminded on the absence of pain.

Trials and tests are very often painful situations. They make you aware of your need of healing and restoration, towards the person God intended you to be. We always try to solve our problems on our own strength, but in God's trials and testing, that will never work. In the trials and testing, our strength, knowledge, insight and wisdom are insufficient to solve the matter. Why? Because they have the aim to teach you to become dependent on God again, like mankind was when He created us. We need to become aware of how insufficient we are and that we can do nothing without God, as Jesus clearly stated.

I am the vine, you are the branches. He who abides in Me, and I in him, bears much fruit; for without Me you can do nothing.
John 15:5

During trials and tests, this becomes painfully clear. Especially when everything you do seems to fail. It makes you realize that you really can't do a thing without Jesus. The further you go, the more that awareness grows. Until the point you have learned not to start on your own strength, but to start with presenting the matter to Jesus and to ask for His instructions on how to deal with it. Then we have to learn to obey His instructions and to act accordingly, no matter how unlikely or strange the instructions may sound. Yes, you will experience failure in that process. Many believe that the aim is to have success, while that is not the aim of God. It is His aim to shape your character, to teach you to be totally dependent on Him and to teach you not to give up, no matter what. Whether that's accomplished by you succeeding or by you failing, that is really of no concern. But when we've reached the finish of these trials and tests, the pain will go away and the awareness will go with it. That is when the test of "success" begins.

When the test of "success" begins, your life suddenly changes. Suddenly all the doors to success are opened. Now let me start by telling you that when (not if) this happens to you, that means God says you're ready for that test. You're not going into this unequipped. When this starts to happen, it means you have all the means necessary to succeed the test. But you need to apply all the lessons that you have learned, in order to remain standing. You may have incredible successes, while slowly drifting away from being dependent on God. You are aware of pain, but when there is no pain to be aware of, life seems to become a matter of course, something that is obvious. For example, when you're in need of money, you ask God to help you. When you have a filled bank account, you just go to the ATM, while you should do the same. Your time, money and all your possessions belong to God. So He should decide what happens. But when we have a filled bank account, we already have access to all the funding's. At such a moment it's hard to stay dependent. The same applies to everything else God gives you. If you have received the gift of healing, you can pray for the sick and they will be healed. Because God is faithful to His Word. But even in that situation you can easily lose your dependency. When it happens anyway, the need to pray and to listen to His voice seems to become less, while the need stays exactly the same. We need to stay alert at all times, aware of our need of Jesus, while continuing to stay dependent on Him. No matter how successful we are or will be. Be prepared for these traps, for falling is way too easy.

THE ANOINTING KILLERS
Whenever we talk about walking, it is inevitable that we also fall now and then. Whenever we learn something from the Word of God, He

will give us the necessary revelations, wisdom and insight, in order to understand what He wants to teach us. As soon as we've understood it, there is only one thing that can make our faith real and strong: testing. Many times God allows situations to happen in our lives, to show us that something does or does not work. The very first example of that can be found at the beginning of Genesis, when God said: "It is not good that man should be alone". He already knew that Adam needed a woman, but the one who didn't knew that was Adam. And so God proved His point.

Out of the ground the Lord God formed every beast of the field and every bird of the air, and brought them to Adam to see what he would call them. And whatever Adam called each living creature, that was its name. So Adam gave names to all cattle, to the birds of the air, and to every beast of the field. But for Adam there was not found a helper comparable to him. **Genesis 2:19-20**

God wasn't confused or surprised when Adam came to the conclusion that there was no helper to be found for him, that was comparable to him. Before God started to create all the other living creatures, Adam wasn't aware of his need. Afterwards, and while God was watching how he would call all the animals, Adam was very aware of his need. When he reached that point, that was the moment God created the woman. Because at that point, Adam knew how to value her.

The true value of God's gifts only becomes of any value to us when we are able to see our need of it. That applied in the case of Adam. When he received Eve from God, he knew exactly what he had received and how valuable she was. The same also applies to grace. We can only value grace, when we are able to see that carnal condition of our hearts and when we see how sin has ruined our lives. God will never show us our sinful heart to accuse or condemn us. That is what the devil does. He wants you to feel guilty, to feel hopeless and to move away from God. But God shows you your sinful heart, in order to show you your need of Him. And as soon as you realize that, He does the impossible and gives you a brand new heart. Because as soon as you understand your carnal condition, you will know how to value a new heart and how to value the Giver of that heart.

In every lesson there is room for error. It is not God's aim to make you fall or to make you sin. He hates sin and He doesn't want you to fall. But the reality is that sometimes we do fall. When a child learns how to ride a bike, it goes with falling and trying again. And again. And again. Until, at one point, the child knows how to maneuver the bike, in order not to fall but to move ahead. And even then it is still possible that the child falls, even though it will become much less often. It is the same in our walk with God. If you've never fallen, you've never moved. Many Christians spent their lives in Churches where they never move an inch. Thirty or forty years later, they're still precisely the same, doing the same things. They haven't changed further. Most of them haven't been encouraged to do so either. While it may feel much safer not to move and to stick to the known patterns and traditions, it is one of the most deadly things for your Christian life. The Word of God has called us to create disciples, to teach people to start moving. Not just in any direction, but towards the image of Jesus. We are all called to preach the gospel, to speak with new tongues, to cast out demons, to heal the sick etc. That means moving in faith. But the greatest qualities of all are to do justly, to love mercy, and to walk humbly with your God. Without those qualities, all other things become useless. But with those qualities, the spiritual Anointing shall be with you and signs and miracles will follow you, not the other way around. Maybe you're called for the salvation of one person, maybe you're called for the salvation of a million people. It is all just as valuable to God, as long as it comes from a humble and depended heart.

Having said all that, we can now deal with what I call the "Anointing killers". Doing justly, loving mercy and being humble do all come from one place: the heart. My favorite Bible teacher, Derek Prince, once said: "If you want to have a good life, have a good heart". I couldn't agree more. But I can also add something to that. If you want to have an Anointed life, where the spiritual Anointing of our Lord Jesus Christ is in you and surrounds you, the heart is where you need to start. Doing justly, loving mercy and being humble are visible things, but they are not the aim. They are the result, the fruits, of a heart that is righteous, merciful and humble towards God. When the condition of the heart becomes bad, the Anointing goes away. The very first indicator that something is wrong, is the lack of Anointing. Why is God doing that? To make us aware that something is wrong. From that point the situation will become worse and worse, until we finally realize that at some point we've gone in the wrong direction.

"I blasted you with blight and mildew. When your gardens increased, your vineyards, your fig trees, and your olive trees, the locust devoured them; Yet you have not returned to Me," says the Lord.
Amos 4:9

God can and does that. Not for your destruction, not with the aim to condemn you, but to give you another chance to return to Him, while there is still time. That means that the Anointing can be restored, if we respond in a proper way.

The cause of the lack of Anointing can be described in one word: Pride. It is the root of every other sin. And it will instantly kill the Anointing. What remains are death works of man. The Bible teaches us that satan accuses us wherever and whenever he gets the chance. The enemy will try to overload us with feelings of guilt and shame, whenever we commit sin. But there is one exception. For he will never accuse you of pride. He will never make you feel guilty or ashamed because of pride. Because he doesn't consider it to be a sin. And because it would be an admission of his own sin, for it was his pride that caused him to be banned from the presence of God. Because of his pride, he no longer is the Anointed Cherub, but a person who was stripped of his identity and Anointing. The lack of accusation also makes it dangerous. When we don't feel guilty, we often think that nothing is wrong. We often use that as our only indicator, but when we do that, we miss the most important sin of all, which is the sin of pride. When God takes His distance, when the Anointing lacks, that's the moment to pay attention. A very clear and detailed description of this can be found in 2 Chronicles, where it speaks about the life of Hezekiah, the king of Judah.

In those days Hezekiah was sick and near death, and he prayed to the Lord; and He spoke to him and gave him a sign. But Hezekiah did not repay according to the favor shown him, for his heart was lifted up; therefore wrath was looming over him and over Judah and Jerusalem. Then

Hezekiah humbled himself for the pride of his heart, he and the inhabitants of Jerusalem, so that the wrath of the Lord did not come upon them in the days of Hezekiah.
2 Chronicles 32:24-26

Hezekiah was one of the Lord's Anointed. He was the king of Judah. In his time of need and sickness, God answered him. But his heart became prideful, causing the wrath of God to come over him and over everyone and everything that was under his authority. No blessings, no presence of God and no spiritual Anointing. The exact opposite started to happen. But then the king saw his mistake and acted as a man of God should act. He humbled himself, along with all the people, and God answered again and completely restored him in every little detail. The blessings returned, God's presence returned and the spiritual Anointing returned. As a result there was also great riches of spices and oil in the natural, as can be seen in the verses 27 and 28.

To be or not to be humble is a matter of choice. It has nothing to do with emotion or feelings. It's all about attitude. You can choose to be humble in your heart, but you can also allow pride in your heart. But one thing is for sure. Pride goes before destruction, a haughty spirit before a fall (Proverbs 16:18). The moment you allow pride in your heart is the moment your destiny is set. Unless you change your ways. Pride is everything you do from the desire to be independent of God and to lean on your own wisdom, knowledge and understanding. There are only a very few Bible verses that specifically mention the works of pride that will cause the Anointing to stop, but the following verse is the most specific of all.

You shall sow, but not reap; you shall tread the olives, but not anoint yourselves with oil; and make sweet wine, but not drink wine. For the statutes of Omri are kept; all the works of Ahab's house are done; and you walk in their counsels, that I may make you a desolation, and your inhabitants a hissing. Therefore you shall bear the reproach of My people.
Micah 6:15

The biggest Anointing killers that the Bible makes mention of are the works of Omri and the works of his son Ahab (who married Jezebel, a servant of Baal). The root sin of all was and is pride, but it caused many other sins as well, such as sexual sins, self-exaltation, self-promotion, unrightfully gaining authority, worshiping idols, witchcraft, persecution of God's Anointed servants etc. For this reason, Jesus also warned the Church in Thyatira against it (Revelation 2:20). Jesus describes all these works specifically as the knowledge of "the depths of satan" (verse 24). Also note that from the outside, everything seemed perfect. Jesus said: "I know your works, love, service, faith, and your patience; and as for your works, the last are more than the first." What does it take in order to see the problem? Revelation. What is the first sign that something is wrong? When the Anointing stops and lacks. When that happens it is time to pay very much attention. The way back to the Anointing is to humble yourself, starting in your heart.

And all the churches shall know that I am He who searches the minds and hearts.
Revelation 2:23

FALLEN ANOINTED LEADERS
Leaders rise and leaders fall. The Anointed leaders are no exception. But what distinguishes them from all other leaders is not that they do not fall, but that they respond differently if or when it happens. Many people believe that Anointed leaders only have one chance to do it right. As soon as an Anointed leader falls, they don't know how fast to wash their hands in 'innocence', while publically keeping their distance from that person. But that's not a response from the Spirit of God, that's a response from the political spirit, the enemy of God. That kind of attitude and response has the aim to destroy a person and ministry. Jesus said that we can know a person by his fruits (Matthew 7:20). He also told us what the fruits of our enemy are, which are to steal, to kill and to destroy (John 10:10). Every person that shows the same fruits, shows which master he is following. The aim and the fruits of God are to save, to heal, to deliver and to restore. Each of His true followers will show the exact same fruits.

When an Anointed leader falls, I always look at the fruits they are showing. I'm not talking about their sin, for we all had sin in our lives and we all know how easily it ensnares us (Hebrews 12:1). I'm talking about their response when it happens. For their response will tell me everything about their walk with Jesus and their love for Jesus.

Let the righteous strike me; It shall be a kindness. And let him rebuke me; It shall be as excellent oil; Let my head not refuse it.
Psalm 141:5

God doesn't tolerate sin. Neither does He approve it in any way. But He is a merciful God. He is a restoring God. More than that, He longs for us, He longs to restore us, He longs to be close to us. He desires a heart to heart relationship. Therefore He will closely watch the condition of our heart, when we respond to sin. There may be sin in our hearts, but as long as there still is a humble attitude towards God, and the willingness to plead guilty, God has enough to work with to restore us. The difference in the condition of heart can be compared with the responses of Saul and David, when both were confronted with their sins. The response of Saul started with "Yes, but…", while David didn't dare to justify himself and pleaded guilty immediately. He didn't justify himself, but responded in a way a man of God responds.

So David said to Nathan, "I have sinned against the Lord."
2 Samuel 12:13

and David fasted and went in and lay all night on the ground. So the elders of his house arose and went to him, to raise him up from the ground. But he would not, nor did he eat food with them.
2 Samuel 12:16-17

So David arose from the ground, washed and anointed himself, and changed his clothes; and he went into the house of the Lord and worshiped.
2 Samuel 12:20

Because of David's humble and sincere response to his sin, God restored him completely. His position was not taken away. His Anointing was not taken away. Saul responded by justifying his deeds and did not acknowledge his sins in his heart. For that reason his sins were not pardoned and his kingship was taken away from him. Nowadays many let the Saul's of today remain king, while rejecting the David's. The attitude towards sin tells you everything about a person. Although David appeared weak and vulnerable when he dealt with his sin, his name was and is remembered in honor, while Saul… Well, we know how that ended. Whenever we deal with people, we deal with human error. The way we deal with that says a lot about who we are and who we serve. Is it the likeness of Jesus? Or the likeness and depths of the enemy? Jesus doesn't tolerate sin, deals radically with those who are not willing to repent, but is extremely merciful to those who plead guilty. He will meet them in their weakness and despair, and He will restore them in honor. The enemy will tolerate sin, will accept the excuses and justification of sinful deeds, but is extremely judgmental to those who plead guilty, seeking to destroy them. These fruits will tell you everything about the source its coming from.

OPPOSITION AGAINST THE ANOINTING
Wherever and whenever the spiritual Anointing starts to flow, there is always opposition. No matter where you look in the history of the people of Israel and the history of the Church, you'll see it everywhere. If you haven't met any resistance or opposition, you might want to reconsider the road you're on. How does the enemy oppose against us? He has two very effective weapons against the Anointing.

Then He charged them, saying, "Take heed, beware of the leaven of the Pharisees and the leaven of Herod."
Mark 8:15

When Jesus talks about the leaven of the Pharisees and the leaven of Herod, He talks about the religious spirit and the political spirit. Both enemies of the Anointing. Both putting their trust in their own efforts and rules, pretending to be righteous and holy, but being far from it. The use of leaven was strictly forbidden in all offerings made to the Lord by fire. Neither can the religious spirit or the political spirit stand the test of God's holy fire, for all these spirits do is justifying themselves. It is like trying to live for God, without Him being involved. It looks very honorable, even very religious, but it has no meaning at all. These powers even want to go as far as killing to get the people on their side, to protect their own belief system, rules and traditions. An example of this can be seen in the life of Jesus, Who constantly had to deal with these powers.

"I know that you are Abraham's descendants, but you seek to kill Me, because My word has no place in you. I speak what I have seen with My Father, and you do what you have seen with your father."
John 8:37-38

Now a great many of the Jews knew that He was there; and they came, not for Jesus' sake only, but that they might also see Lazarus, whom He had raised from the dead. But the chief priests plotted to put Lazarus to death also, because on account of him many of the Jews went away and believed in Jesus.
John 12:9-11

They may be believers, but they aren't Christians. They may believe that the Word of God is true, but so does satan. Only those who abide in the Words of Jesus are His true disciples (John 8:31). It's not enough to go to Bible school, to attend Church every Sunday and to know every Word from the Bible. Let me ensure you that satan knows every Word as well. He probably knows it better than most Christians. But without the insight, revelation and wisdom, the Word has no value. Like it or not, we are dependent on God. We are blind, until He enables us to see. Only those who ask will receive. Only those who search with their whole heart will find. Only those who keep on knocking, without giving up, will see the door be opened to them. But to each and every one who are using the Word as a means to justify themselves, all wisdom and insight will be withheld. They wouldn't recognize the truth if it was right in front of them. They will never be able to produce the fruits of the Spirit or to act in the Anointing, for darkness is not able to produce any anointing (James 3:12).

For by grace you have been saved through faith, and that not of yourselves; it is the gift of God, not of works, lest anyone should boast.
Ephesians 2:8-9

The Anointing will always unite the true followers of Jesus Christ (Psalm 133). It will never divide, but gather. Where the Anointing falls, there is instant unity among the true Christians, no matter their differences. The Holy Spirit in you will never attack another person with the Holy Spirit. The Holy Spirit cannot and will not work against Himself. But any spirit other than the Holy Spirit will attack the Anointing.

Jesus said to them, "If God were your Father, you would love Me, for I proceeded forth and came from God; nor have I come of Myself, but He sent Me. Why do you not understand My speech? Because you are not able to listen to My word. You are of your father the devil, and the desires of your father you want to do. He was a murderer from the beginning, and does not stand in the truth, because there is no truth in him. When he speaks a lie, he speaks from his own resources, for he is a liar and the father of it. But because I tell the truth, you do not believe Me.
John 8:42-45

So you want the spiritual Anointing? You want to walk, talk and act in it? Go for it! God encourages you to go after that. But do know that when Jesus faced opposition, while walking, talking and acting in the Anointing, that so will you. A student is not above his Teacher, nor a servant above his Master (Matthew 10:24). How can you remain standing? Abide in His Word. Read it, meditate on it, search for the insight and wisdom behind it and live it.

"Therefore do not fear them. For there is nothing covered that will not be revealed, and hidden that will not be known. Whatever I tell you in the dark, speak in the light; and what you hear in the ear, preach on the housetops. And do not fear those who kill the body but cannot kill the soul. But rather fear Him who is able to destroy both soul and body in hell. Are not two sparrows sold for a copper coin? And not one of them falls to the ground apart from your Father's will. But the very hairs of your head are all numbered. Do not fear therefore; you are of more value than many sparrows.
Matthew 10:26-31

CHAPTER 11
ANOINTED WORSHIP

While the Word of God is the only thing that has the power to change you from the inside out, it will also prepare you on when and how to deal with the Anointing. For the Anointing of God, the spiritual Anointing, is not something to be used based on our own insight. It is the Word of God that equips you, it is the Spirit of God Who makes it alive in you. But the way to access the Anointing is through worship. Many believe that worship is just singing some songs, maybe even some nice songs, but it is more than that. It is a lifestyle. It can be described as a state of heart. A state of dependency. The Word can be in you and it can be alive in you. But then you need to do something with it. In other words, how do you respond? If you know the Truth, which is Jesus Christ, then how will that affect your life? If it does nothing, it is worthless. We need to do something with it, so we need to come in action. We need to allow the Word to apply God's changes in our lives and we need to respond to the work of the Holy Spirit and the Holy Word in us. That can be done through a lifestyle of worship.

The people of Israel were used to many rituals and customs, in order to serve God. In those times, the presence of God was only to be found in the Temple, and before that in the Tabernacle. So basically, there was no direct contact between God and His people. The priests were the ones who were allowed to come into God's presence and to act on behalf of the people. And then, when all of that still applied, and before Jesus died on the cross, He made the following statement, which was very remarkable for that time.

Jesus said to her, "Woman, believe Me, the hour is coming when you will neither on this mountain, nor in Jerusalem, worship the Father. You worship what you do not know; we know what we worship, for salvation is of the Jews. But the hour is coming, and now is, when the true worshipers will worship the Father in spirit and truth; for the Father is seeking such to worship Him. God is Spirit, and those who worship Him must worship in

spirit and truth."
John 4:21-24

God is Spirit. He lives in the spiritual realm. Everything He does, happens in the spiritual realm first, before we see any results in our natural and visible realm. The Tabernacle and the Temple were the gateway to and connection with God in those days, but only through the priests, not directly. When Jesus died on the cross, that all changed. From the moment the veil was torn, God left the Temple and chose us, the followers and disciples of Jesus Christ, as His residence. He now lives in us. His presence lives in us. But He is still Spirit. No spiritual matter can ever be approached in a natural way. We deal with natural matters on a natural way, and we deal with spiritual matters on a spiritual way. Jesus made it clear that we do not serve a natural god, but a supernatural One, a God Who is Spirit. Therefore we must worship in spirit. But notice that it also says "in truth". That is the second condition. The truth of God must live in our hearts, the source of all our thoughts and acts. This is the basis of repentance, which literally means 'to change your mind'. We must bring our hearts back in line with the Word of God. This means that when God considers something to be a sin, we consider it a sin as well. And when God considers something to be righteous, we consider it righteous as well.

These people draw near to Me with their mouth, and honor Me with their lips, but their heart is far from Me. And in vain they worship Me, teaching as doctrines the commandments of men.
Matthew 15:8-9

What Jesus meant was that there are many people who live very religiousy, who even put yokes on people, by instructing them to keep a set of rules, while the Word doesn't live inside their hearts. With their mouths they tell people what is and what isn't a sin, while in their hearts they still consider sin as an option. Sometimes these people may be able to restrain themselves, to not actually commit the sin by deeds, while they have committed it many times in their minds. To Jesus that is just as bad as actually doing it. For it means that their hearts, where the thoughts are coming from, are living in sin and are far from Him. These people are worshiping Him in vain. These people will never experience the Anointing. More than that, these people usually oppose against the Anointing. So Jesus had a very good reason to add "in truth" to it, for anything that is not in the truth will always work against the Kingdom. To allow or not to allow sin in our hearts is a choice. Some people secretly long for sins or are longing back to their old lives, while others long to become more holy and more free. It all starts with changing our minds in regard to sin, which is what the word 'repentance' means. It needs to start in our hearts.

We need to worship the Father in spirit and in Truth. I'm writing this with a capital letter, because the Truth is not only the Word of God, we also know that our Lord Jesus Christ is the Truth as well. So we can also say that we need to worship in spirit and in Jesus. To some of you that may give a whole new meaning to "No one comes to the Father except through Me", as Jesus said in John 14:6. When we live in the Truth, when the Truth is in our hearts and when we acknowledge the Truth, then we are in the Truth, then we are in Jesus and we are abiding in His Word. We may fall, but we get up again. We may fall, but we'll never justify our sins. But how do we worship in spirit and in Truth?

When you realized that you need Jesus and when you accepted Him as your Messiah and Lord, God removed your old spirit, which was never able to connect with God, and He gave you a brand new spirit (Ezekiel 36:26). That part of us can never be restored, for the decay has already set in. But it can be replaced with a brand new one, which happens when we come to acknowledge Jesus Christ as the Messiah, as our Lord and as the Son of the Living God. That new spirit that you have received is perfectly capable of connecting with God, for it is blameless. But there is a divine route we have to go. Although God's presence left the earthly temple, and although we are the temple that He dwells in right now, there still is a Heavenly Temple in place (Revelation 11:19). This is the route for worship in spirit and in Truth, but it is also the route to a lifestyle of worship in spirit and in Truth. When we follow God's principles, which we meet on this route, we are giving honor to His name. It is the only way to the spiritual Anointing.

CONFESSION OF SINS

Upon entering the Temple, the very first thing we meet is the Bronze Altar or the Altar of sacrifice. This is the place where we are confronted with our sins, which was once a huge blockade for us, to enter into God's presence or to even come near to it. But He dealt with that issue for once and for all.

For God so loved the world that He gave His only begotten Son, that whoever believes in Him should not perish but have everlasting life.
John 3:16

Sin no longer has to hinder us to come into His presence, but it has to be dealt with. It doesn't automatically disappear. The biggest issue God has with His people is the fact that many do not consider their sins to be a sin, while justifying their sinful behavior. You know the type of people I'm talking about. They are the ones who always find excuses to continue with their lifestyle and who are not willing to change anything about it, for it would cost them. There is a group of people who calls themselves Christian, but who want to follow God on their own terms, not on His. That is nothing new, because these kind of people were present in every era. But God has a serious problem with these people. Ignoring your sins or justifying them will cause the presence of God and the Anointing to go away.

I will return again to My place till they acknowledge their offense. Then they will seek My face; In their affliction they will earnestly seek Me.
Hosea 5:15

This verse literally says "till they plead guilty". So how do you plead? We must never forget that Jesus Christ is not only our Savior, He is also our Judge. So how do you plead before Judge Jesus? Guilty? Or not guilty?

If we say that we have no sin, we deceive ourselves, and the truth is not in us. If we confess our sins, He is faithful and just to forgive us our sins and to cleanse us from all unrighteousness. If we say that we have not sinned, we make Him a liar, and His word is not in us.
1 John 1:8-10

I even go a step further. If we say we have no sin, Jesus is not in us. He is the Truth. In that case we are in serious danger of eternal condemnation. For if we refuse to admit sins, that equals to saying that Jesus Christ is a liar. But when we do plead guilty before our Savior and Judge, we are in line with His Word. As you can see in the verse from Hosea, God does not have the aim to condemn. The reason why His presence and Anointing is going away is for us to notice that something is wrong. It has the aim that we are going to seek His face, to find out what is wrong, to deal with it and to have His presence and Anointing back among us. Without His presence and Anointing, all you have left is a worthless religion.

FORGIVENESS AND CLEANSING

The second item we meet in the Temple is the Bronze Laver. This was the place where the priests had to cleanse themselves. In the spiritual realm it is the place where we need to be cleansed as well. When we have dealt with our sins in the way that God wants us to deal with them, by pleading guilty and by confessing our sins, then this is the place where our sins are forgiven and where we are cleansed from all unrighteousness, as if it never happened.

But if we walk in the light as He is in the light, we have fellowship with one another, and the blood of Jesus Christ His Son cleanses us from all sin.
1 John 1:7

This is He who came by water and blood—Jesus Christ; not only by water, but by water and blood. And it is the Spirit who bears witness, because the Spirit is truth.
1 John 5:6

Let us draw near with a true heart in full assurance of faith, having our hearts sprinkled from an evil conscience and our bodies washed with pure water.
Hebrews 10:22

When you deal with your sins thoroughly, Jesus will cleanse you thoroughly. If you plead guilty with your whole heart, your whole heart will be cleansed. And God will never remind you of that sin anymore.

THANKSGIVING AND ACCLAMATION

Because of the sacrifice of Jesus Christ and because He cleansed us thoroughly, we can now enter into His presence and Anointing. The Temple is the Anointed place, as you may remember from previous chapters. Each and every item is Anointed in there, including the doors, door posts etc. So when we've past the Bronze Altar and the Bronze Laver, we are at the entrance of God's spiritual Temple. The way to enter the Holy Place is by thanksgiving and acclamation.

Enter into His gates with thanksgiving, and into His courts with praise. Be thankful to Him, and bless His name.
Psalm 100:4

The Hebrew words literally says that we enter His gates by acclamation. That is the expression of a thankful heart, for the salvation and the forgiveness of sin, and it is the acknowledgement and approval of His Kingship over us.

The voice of rejoicing and salvation is in the tents of the righteous; The right hand of the Lord does valiantly. The right hand of the Lord is exalted; The right hand of the Lord does valiantly. I shall not die, but live, and declare the works of the Lord. The Lord has chastened me severely, but He has not given me over to death. Open to me the gates of righteousness; I will go through them, and I will praise the Lord. This is the gate of the Lord, through which the righteous shall enter. I will praise You, for You have answered me, and have become my salvation.
Psalm 118:15-21

PRAISE HIS NAME

Once we have actually entered His spiritual Temple, by thanksgiving and acclamation, we are walking in the courts of heaven. This is the Holy Place. David says that we walk through His courts with praise, which is a celebration. It is a joyful thing, not a funeral service. The way God's people express their praises to the King of kings is by shouting, clapping their hands, dancing and by raising their hands. These genuine gestures and expressions of praise and celebration can all be found in the Scriptures as part of the normal praises of the people.

The Lord his God is with him, and the shout of a King is among them.
Numbers 23:21

Oh, clap your hands, all you peoples! Shout to God with the voice of triumph! For the Lord Most High is awesome; He is a great King over all the earth.
Psalm 47:1-2

Now it was told King David, saying, "The Lord has blessed the house of Obed-Edom and all that belongs to him, because of the ark of God." So David went and brought up the ark of God from the house of Obed-Edom to the City of David with gladness. And so it was, when those bearing the ark of the Lord had gone six paces, that he sacrificed oxen and fatted sheep. Then David danced before the Lord with all his might; and David was wearing a linen ephod.
2 Samuel 6:12-14

Because Your lovingkindness is better than life, my lips shall praise You. Thus I will bless You while I live; I will lift up my hands in Your name.
Psalm 63:3-4

We have lost so many of these expressions, out of the fear of man and their opinions. But this is the time of restoration. Don't try to curb the joy inside of you, but give God the praises and honor that He is due.

BLESS HIS NAME IN WORSHIP

At the end of the Holy Place, right before you go through the veil, is the Altar of Incense. This is the place where all our praises and celebrations fade to worship. The incense stands for prayer, intercession and worship. The most beautiful example of what that is like in Heaven, can be found in Revelation.

Now when He had taken the scroll, the four living creatures and the twenty-four elders fell down before the Lamb, each having a harp, and golden bowls full of incense, which are the prayers of the saints.
Revelation 5:8

The offerings made on the Altar of Incense are offerings made to God by fire. The prayers and intercession are going along with the worship, as we can see from the same scene in Heaven. Right after the incense of our prayers are offered to Jesus, the whole of Heaven burst out in worship. The book of Revelation says that they all start to sing a new song to Jesus.

You are worthy to take the scroll, and to open its seals; For You were slain, and have redeemed us to God by Your blood out of every tribe and tongue and people and nation, and have made us kings and priests to our God; and we shall reign on the earth.

Worthy is the Lamb who was slain to receive power and riches and wisdom, and strength and honor and glory and blessing!

Blessing and honor and glory and power be to Him who sits on the throne, and to the Lamb, forever and ever!
Revelation 5:9,10,12,13

When we offer our worship to the Lord, in spirit and in Truth, the spiritual Anointing will start to flow. This is the moment when we stand in front of the mercy seat of Christ, where He is enthroned. That mercy seat is based on top of the Ark of the Covenant or the Ark of Testimony. We enter the Holy of Holies through the veil, that is the flesh of Jesus, and are coming before the mercy seat through worship. That is when our spirit is in front of our Savior, Master and King, our Messiah Jesus. The Anointed One. Yeshua HaMashiach. That is the moment when we give Him all the blessing and honor.

Many Churches do understand how to get there. Many worship leaders and worship teams do understand how to get there. But the majority does not understand what to do there. I've been in so many Churches where the congregation was being led in actual worship in spirit and in Truth. But just when the Anointing would start to flow, they always would stop. Time for the sermon. And another missed chance. If they would have pushed through, they would have had so much Anointing. Derek Prince once nailed it when he said: "It is like taking an airplane to a destination, only to return upon arrival." Then why are we going there in the first place? Why all the effort? I don't know about you, but I don't need religious exercise, I need the Anointing. I need the Anointed One. He is our destination when we worship. So why not spending some time when we finally arrive there? Don't care about those who stare at their watches during the service. The service is meant for Jesus, not for the congregation. If you want the blessing and the spiritual Anointing, it pays to spend more time in worship and adoration. Worship with our fullest attention and focus on Jesus.

The worship is the most important thing in God's Temple. The priests were to offer the incense first, before they filled the lamps with new oil. No other offerings but worship are accepted. He wants all of us. All of our time, all of our focus and all of our attention. That's what He paid for at Calvary. He paid for all of you, not for just a part. And when He has received the blessing and honor and glory and power that He is due, then we can fill our lamps with His oil. And there is plenty of oil available.

Anointing is like a river. It needs to flow. When we stop sharing it, the Anointing will stop as well. As long as we share, it will remain flowing. We can go there through worship, whether the worship means singing songs, or whether we live the worship in our hearts. No one can touch the Anointed One and leave unchanged, like no one can touch the oil, without having traces of oil on their hands. In His presence, everything changes. One minute under the Anointing can do way more than years of striving on our own effort.

Therefore, brethren, having boldness to enter the Holiest by the blood of Jesus, by a new and living way which He consecrated for us, through the veil, that is, His flesh, and having a High Priest over the house of God, let us draw near with a true heart in full assurance of faith, having our hearts sprinkled from an evil conscience and our bodies washed with pure water.
Hebrews 10:19-22

Seeing then that we have a great High Priest who has passed through the heavens, Jesus the Son of God, let us hold fast our confession. For we do not have a High Priest who cannot sympathize with our weaknesses, but was in all points tempted as we are, yet without sin. Let us therefore come

boldly to the throne of grace, that we may obtain mercy and find grace to help in time of need.
Hebrews 4:14-16

CHAPTER 12

THE MEANING OF ANOINTING OIL FRAGRANCES

The Word of God is not just a random collection of words, even though the order of some Bible books have been changed throughout the years, and even though parts were left out. When God speaks, He carefully weighs each and every word He says. He never says a word too much or too little. Each Word has a meaning and a message for us in these days, even though it may sometimes look random. The fact that 201 chapters and 345 verses in the Word of God are speaking about the oil, and the fact that the term 'Anointed One', which is the translation for Messiah, appears 596 times, tells us that there are almost 1000 Bible verses, where God wants to teach us something about the Anointing and the Anointing Oil. Why else would Jesus be called the Messiah? If His name would have meant "Son of God" it would have been great as well. But He is called the Anointed One. Not because it has such a nice sound, but because it means something.

Most of the Anointing Oils in the Bible were fragrant oils. But all of the Anointing Oils that were used for the service of the Lord were fragrant oils. As we have seen, the Anointing in the natural is a prophetic deed of empowerment by the Holy Spirit, of the glory of God and of holiness. But we haven't covered the fragrances of the oil yet. Each fragrance of the Anointing Oils has a specific prophetic meaning as well.

Many places in the Bible are referring to ointments and fragrances. Two examples are the following verses.

Because of the fragrance of your good ointments, Your name is ointment poured forth; Therefore the virgins love you.
Song of Solomon 1:3

Now thanks be to God who always leads us in triumph in Christ, and

through us diffuses the fragrance of His knowledge in every place. For we are to God the fragrance of Christ among those who are being saved and among those who are perishing. To the one we are the aroma of death leading to death, and to the other the aroma of life leading to life.
2 Corinthians 2:14-16

We know that Jesus, to Whom the text of Song of Solomon is referring, is in the spiritual realm. We know that His fragrance, where both Bible parts are referring to, can be smelled in the spiritual realm. To us that fragrance means life. To every creature that does not belong to Jesus it means death. The whole spiritual realm is very aware of the fragrance of Christ. His fragrance and glory are going before Him. When a spirit, that is not from God, smells His fragrance, he trembles and flees. When we use fragrances in the natural world, it is a prophetic deed of what already took place in the spiritual realm, but has not yet become visible in our natural realm. By Anointing someone with a fragrant oil, we show our faith in what Christ has already done for us. These are the prophetic meanings of the fragrances that are used in the Anointing Oils.

FRANKINCENSE & MYRRH – HEALING & INTERCESSION
In temple days, sweet incense containing Frankincense was placed on the Inner Altar of the Tabernacle and burned morning and evening. It speaks of intercession. Myrrh, used as a burial spice and in purification rites, was a primary ingredient of the Holy Anointing Oil. It speaks of suffering and death, but our total deliverance in the atoning work of Messiah. Frankincense & Myrrh, two of the three prophetic gifts given to the Messiah at His birth, represent His role as Priest and Prophet, signifying all that Messiah would do and continues to do on our behalf.

"He was wounded for our transgression, He was bruised for our iniquities; ....and by His stripes we are healed."
Isaiah 53:5

"...he is totally able to deliver those who approach God through him; since he is alive forever and thus able to intercede on their behalf."
Hebrews 7:24-2

This is probably one of the most effective fragrances that can be used for prayer for deliverance. As I've said before, the spiritual realm runs parallel to the natural realm. It means that what we see in this natural world, is a result of what already took place in the spiritual realm. In the spiritual and in the natural realm, snakes hate this fragrance. Just the smell of this fragrance often leads to manifestations. In Israel these fragrances were often used to keep snakes away from under the houses.

CASSIA – DEDICATION & DEVOTION
Cassia was one of the principal spices of the Holy Anointing oil used to anoint priests, kings and their garments. Likewise, the coming King Messiah's robes will smell of cassia. Cassia is not frequently used today but was apparently a highly valued commodity in biblical times. The root word, kiddah, in both Hebrew and Arabic, signifies a strip and refers to the strips of bark from which the spice is made. In the spiritual sense, cassia speaks of devotion (being stripped of pride) and consecration (set apart) with a servant's heart. The deep, exotic aroma and the rich color of our Cassia oil make it a welcome addition to our family of biblical fragrant anointing oils.

"Your robes are all fragrant with myrrh, aloes and cassia..."
Psalm 45:8

CEDARS OF LEBANON – STRENGTH & PROTECTION
The cedar of Lebanon is a huge evergreen tree by Middle Eastern standards, reaching 90 feet in height, the "King" of all biblical trees. The wood is astonishingly decay-resistant and it is never eaten by insect larvae. It is beautifully majestic and red-toned with deep green leaves. The tree bark is dark gray and exudes a gumlike resin from which the highly aromatic oils are produced. Cedars of Lebanon is the strong, fragrant wood used to build David's house, Solomon's house and much of the First Temple. It was also used along with hyssop in the cleansing of a leper's house. It speaks of strength, permanence, wholeness and restoration.

"The righteous shall flourish like the palm tree: he shall grow like a cedar in Lebanon."

Psalm 92:12

HYSSOP (HOLY FIRE) – PURIFICATION & EMPOWERMENT

Hyssop is a low growing evergreen, bushy herb growing 1 to 2 feet high, cultivated for its flower tops, from which the fragrance is extracted. The herb grows in arid climates out of rocky soil and out of cracks in ancient walls such as in the old Temple area of Jerusalem. Hyssop was once called a "Holy Herb" because it was used for sprinkling in the ritual practices of the Hebrews. Ex 12:22 reads, "And ye shall take a bunch of hyssop, and dip it in the blood that is in the basin, and strike the lintel and the two side posts." Because of the reference found in Num. 19:6 ("And the priest shall take cedar wood, and hyssop, and scarlet, and cast it into the midst of the burning of the heifer"), we have called this fragrance "HOLY FIRE." Hyssop speaks of spiritual cleansing by the refining fire of the Holy Spirit and can best be described as a "fresh, clean-smelling" aroma.

"Purge me with hyssop, and I shall be clean: wash me, and I shall be whiter than snow."
Psalm 51:7

KING'S GARMENTS – GLORY OF THE KING

In Psalm 45:8 the Bible portrays a king whose garments are so thoroughly scented with costly perfumes that they seem to be altogether woven out of them. Two of the three scents mentioned, Myrrh and Cassia, were ingredients in the holy anointing oil used to anoint priests and kings. The remaining fragrance, Aloes, is listed among the "chief species" in the garden of the beloved in Song 4:13-14. King's Garments is a special aromatic blending of the three biblical scents consisting of:

Myrrh: A gum resin that exudes from a small bushy tree found in Arabia. It flows as milky white then quickly turns to a deep purple-brown color as it begins to crystalize.

Aloes: Most likely the product of a tree of the genus Aquilaria, a native of northern India. At a certain stage of decay, the wood develops a fragrance well known to the ancients and from it a rare perfume was obtained.

Cassia: An evergreen tree in the cinnamon family with an aromatic bark, which is harvested in strips to make an aromatic powder or oil.

MYRRH – GRACE & PEACE
Myrrh, an exotic biblical spice, was used in purification and beautification rites, in the formula for the Holy Anointing Oil, and in burial spices. Queen Esther was bathed in Oil of Myrrh for six months and with other aloes and perfumes for another six months before her presentation to the king. Bitter to the taste but sweet to the smell, myrrh in the spiritual sense speaks of dying to self to become a "sweet smelling savor" to the Lord.

"A bundle of myrrh is my well-beloved unto me."
Song of Sol. 1:13

POMEGRANATE – BLESSING & FAVOR
The pomegranate, a Persian native, is one of the oldest fruits known to man and was highly esteemed by the Israelites. An enormous number of the flower petals must be pressed and steam-distilled in order to make a quantity of oil. Once pressed the slightly amber oil, which is the basis for all our Pomegranate products, gives off a pleasant and slightly fruity odor.

Jewish tradition teaches that the pomegranate is a symbol for righteousness, because it is said to have 613 seeds which correspond with the 613 mitzvot or commandments of the Torah. Pomegranate is one of the seven species the spies brought back with them to show how fertile the Promised Land was. It speaks of God's favor exhibited in fruitfulness and abundance.

"They came to the valley of Eshkol...they brought also of the pomegranates, and of the figs."
Numbers 13:23

ROSE OF SHARON – BEAUTY OF THE BELOVED
The Rose of Sharon fragrance is best described as "tea-rose", a not-too-sweet, light, floral scent, which does not overpower. This flower from

the region of Sharon in Israel is actually not a rose, but is part of the hibiscus family.

Its blooms are nonetheless beautiful and glorious, just as Isaiah depicted the Bride of Messiah would be in the millennial reign when she shines forth in all the radiance of her heavenly glory, beauty, gentleness and honor.

"I am the rose of Sharon, the lily of the valleys."
Song of Sol 2:1

SPIKENARD – WORSHIP & PRAISE

Spikenard, a rare and costly fragrant oil, was used by Mary of Bethany to anoint the head and feet of the Messiah two days before His death, as recorded in John 12:3: "Then Mary took a pound of ointment of spikenard, very costly, and anointed the feet of Jesus, and wiped his feet with her hair: and the house was filled with the odor of the ointment." It speaks of the Bride's extravagant adoration of and intimacy with the Bridegroom, in total abandonment, without regard to cost. It symbolizes the Bride who has made herself ready.

"While the king sits at his table, my spikenard sends forth its fragrance."
Song of Sol 1:12

CINNAMON – PASSION & COURAGE

Sweet Cinnamon is one of the four aromatic ingredients of the Holy Anointing Oil described in Exodus 30:23. The fragrance of cinnamon has a rich full bodied aromatic energy about it once it permeates the atmosphere. Cinnamon added to the holy anointing oil is the seasoning that brings passion and stirs up fire to continue on no matter what the pressure. It represents Holy Boldness, Courage and Passion in the believer.

CHAPTER 13

JESUS CHRIST: THE ANOINTED ONE

In our search through the Bible, to find answers on the Anointing Oil and the Anointing, there is One Person whom we always meet: the Anointed One. His Hebrew name is Yeshua HaMashiach, but in our western world we know Him as Jesus Christ.

Obviously, Jesus was not named Jesus when He was born, for He wasn't born in our western society. Neither was He named Yesous (iEsou), the Greek version of Jesus. He is a Jew. So He received a Jewish Hebrew name, which was Yeshua. Yeshua was a shortened form of the name Yehoshua. The prefix "Yeho" is an abbreviation of the four letter word "Yod-He-Vav-He" or YHVH, the name of God. The second part of the name Yehoshua is a form of the Hebrew verb yasha, which means to deliver, save, or rescue. Together, Yehoshua can be translated as "The God Who saves, rescues and delivers".

The name Mashiach, Messiah, Messias, Christ, Christus or Christou all mean the exact same thing: The Anointed One. Like I've pointed out before, this title was not exclusively used for Jesus. In the Old Testament the prophets were called "messiah's" as well, because they were also Anointed. But there is only One Who can call Himself THE MESSIAH, instead of a messiah. That is Jesus.

Jesus Christ: The Anointed God Who saves, rescues and delivers.

His name shows everything about the intention of God for us, as mankind. He has no desire to see people go towards their destruction, neither does He want to condemn anyone. It is His desire that every human being will get saved, healed, delivered and restored. That was exactly what Jesus said and lived, while He walked on earth. When He was is the synagogue of Nazareth, He revealed this identity to the people who were present.

"The Spirit of the Lord is upon Me, because He has anointed Me to preach the gospel to the poor; He has sent Me to heal the brokenhearted, to proclaim liberty to the captives and recovery of sight to the blind, to set at liberty those who are oppressed; To proclaim the acceptable year of the Lord." Then He closed the book, and gave it back to the attendant and sat down. And the eyes of all who were in the synagogue were fixed on Him. And He began to say to them, "Today this Scripture is fulfilled in your hearing."
Luke 4:18-21

The part that Jesus was reading was coming from the book of Isaiah, that referred to Him. That part actually says a bit more then is mentioned in the book of Luke. This is what is says.

"The Spirit of the Lord God is upon Me, because the Lord has anointed Me to preach good tidings to the poor; He has sent Me to heal the brokenhearted, to proclaim liberty to the captives, and the opening of the prison to those who are bound; To proclaim the acceptable year of the Lord, and the day of vengeance of our God; to comfort all who mourn, to console those who mourn in Zion, to give them beauty for ashes, the oil of joy for mourning, the garment of praise for the spirit of heaviness; that they may be called trees of righteousness, the planting of the Lord, that He may be glorified."
Isaiah 61:1-3

However we look at it, it was an amazing and extraordinary happening. The almighty, all-powerful and omnipresent God, Who humbles Himself to the level of humanity, in order to save us. What a love does He has for us! Wounded for our transgressions. Bruised for our iniquities. The chastisement for our peace was upon Him, and by His stripes we are healed. He carried the punishment that we deserved. Every last bit of it. Nothing was left out. At any moment Jesus had the choice to deny, the choice to back out, which would have been an understandable thing to do. But He didn't. He willingly and knowingly gave Himself for each and every one of us. By doing so He took our sins away and restored our righteousness with His righteousness.

"Your throne, O God, is forever and ever; a scepter of righteousness is

the scepter of Your kingdom. You have loved righteousness and hated lawlessness; therefore God, Your God, has anointed You with the oil of gladness more than Your companions."
Hebrews 1:8-9 / Psalm 45:6-7

Here we see a clear connection between the Anointing and righteousness, which also shows that lawlessness will lead to the disappearance of the Anointing. Lawlessness can basically be described as anything that is not in line with the Words of Jesus Christ. Another way to explain it is doing what we want, without considering the will of God. It may not be a conscious choice, but it comes forth from the human desire to be independent of God, which comes forth from pride. And as we've seen in the previous chapters, pride is the strongest Anointing killer, for it goes directly against the will and character of Jesus Christ. He is the example of humility. He came to serve us, not to rule over us. Nowadays He does rule over us, but in order to get there, He had to serve first. Since His life is the example for our lives, it means that we don't have a different route than He had. We are called to reign into the eons of the eons, together with our Master and the King of kings, Jesus Christ. But the only way to get there is by serving first. Why does the Anointing disappear when we are not in line with the Words of Jesus? Not to punish us, but to make us aware that something is terribly wrong. It has the aim to make us return to dependency and to bring our lives, homes and Churches back in line with the Words of Jesus Christ. Then the Anointing shall return.

The book of Hebrews, which quoted from Psalm 45, describes the Anointing as the "oil of gladness". But what exactly is that? A happy feeling? It is way more than that. It does make you happy, but it is not just that. The book of Acts gives a clear answer to what the Anointing with the Oil of Gladness is exactly.

How God anointed Jesus of Nazareth with the Holy Spirit and with power, who went about doing good and healing all who were oppressed by the devil, for God was with Him.
Acts 10:38

This verse refers to the verses from Luke 4 and Isaiah 61, which we've read before. It makes it crystal clear that the Anointing that is mentioned is the Holy Spirit and the power of the Holy Spirit. That is not just the Holy Spirit in your heart. It is the Holy Spirit in your whole being, as if you are soaked in Him. And on top of that it is the garment of His power. So He lives in every part of you and surrounds you. That is the type of Anointing that Jesus had and has. That is what made Him the Son of Oil. The Anointed One. As One dripping Oil. That same Anointing is available to every believer, to everyone who accepts and acknowledges Jesus Christ as his or her Messiah, Lord and as the Son of God. This is the Anointing where the prophet Isaiah spoke about, when he said the following.

It shall come to pass in that day that his burden will be taken away from your shoulder, and his yoke from your neck, and the yoke will be destroyed because of the anointing oil.
Isaiah 10:27

It is the Holy Spirit, the Spirit of Jesus, the Spirit of Liberty, Who will take your burden away from your shoulder and Who will destroy the yoke from your neck. The same Spirit that surrounded Jesus, that filled every part of His being, is available to you as well.

For all the promises of God in Him are Yes, and in Him Amen, to the glory of God through us. Now He who establishes us with you in Christ and has anointed us is God, who also has sealed us and given us the Spirit in our hearts as a guarantee.
2 Corinthians 1:20-22

Yes, I've said that the Holy Spirit does not just live inside your heart, but He does reside there as well. When He fills every part of your being, that includes your heart. The reason why the heart is specifically mentioned here, is because the heart is described as the root cause of our sins. So if there is any place where we need Him the most, then it is there. The reason why He gave us the Holy Spirit in our hearts as well is because it serves as a guarantee. The reason why this is emphasized is because it is possible to do the works of Jesus, which can only be done with the help of the Holy Spirit, while He is not in the heart. So He can surround a person,

He can even use their hands to perform miracles and deliverances, while the heart remains unchanged. Does that mean that there is such a thing as predestination, a select group of choses ones? In a way, yes. But being a part of that selection does not depend on the status of you, your family or your Church. It does not depend on all the good things you do. It has everything to do with the choices you make with your heart. If you want the Holy Spirit in your heart, He is available to you.

"Not everyone who says to Me, 'Lord, Lord,' shall enter the kingdom of heaven, but he who does the will of My Father in heaven. Many will say to Me in that day, 'Lord, Lord, have we not prophesied in Your name, cast out demons in Your name, and done many wonders in Your name?' And then I will declare to them, 'I never knew you; depart from Me, you who practice lawlessness!'
Matthew 7:21-23

But how is it possible to perform miracles and to cast out demons, when the Holy Spirit is not in the heart? That is because of the name of Jesus. The very same reason why it is possible when He does live in a heart. For each and every miracle and deliverance only takes place, because of Jesus, because of His name and His authority. We have nothing to do with that. It is 100% Jesus Who does it. We just serve as a tool in His hands. Not the other way around. But how can we be sure that we have that guarantee of the Holy Spirit in our hearts as well? That question is answered by Jesus, in the following verses.

"Therefore whoever hears these sayings of Mine, and does them, I will liken him to a wise man who built his house on the rock: and the rain descended, the floods came, and the winds blew and beat on that house; and it did not fall, for it was founded on the rock.
Matthew 7:24-25

If I were to summarize what it means to do the sayings of Jesus, then it would be this: "Love God above everything else, make Him your highest priority. Love your neighbor as yourself, which also means that you have to learn to love yourself in a Godly and healthy way, so that you are able to love another with the love of God. Read His Word, meditate on His

Word, let His Word fill your mind, allow His Word to change your heart and to change your ways. Let the Word of God do the change in you and keep a dependent and humble attitude towards God." It is not about you trying as hard as you can to change yourself. The harder you try, the harder you fail. Only the Word of God has the power to change you from the inside out. The time and effort you need to put into your relationship with Jesus is spending time in His Word, while being focused on Jesus and with the attitude of a student, not of teacher. Ask Him for a teachable spirit and to open up all the knowledge, wisdom and understanding to you. Consider it as a treasure. Ask for it, search for it and don't give up until you have what you came for. Then the next verse will apply to you as well.

But you have an anointing from the Holy One, and you know all things.
1 John 2:20

After we start to know things, we have to do something with them. First in our own lives, as an example, then we have to share it as well. We always receive to share. You receive in an amount that provides for a portion for you and plenty to share. In order to share, you need the Holy Spirit again. You may be a very talented speaker, but you will never be able to communicate with the Anointing and the power of the Holy Spirit, unless it is with His help. Likewise, you may not be a talented speaker at all, but with the help of the Holy Spirit you'll be amazed at what comes out of your mouth. He doesn't ask us to perform as good as possible, He asks us to be dependent and available. Then the Anointing starts to flow.

"For truly against Your holy Servant Jesus, whom You anointed, both Herod and Pontius Pilate, with the Gentiles and the people of Israel, were gathered together to do whatever Your hand and Your purpose determined before to be done. Now, Lord, look on their threats, and grant to Your servants that with all boldness they may speak Your word, by stretching out Your hand to heal, and that signs and wonders may be done through the name of Your holy Servant Jesus." And when they had prayed, the place where they were assembled together was shaken; and they were all filled with the Holy Spirit, and they spoke the word of God with boldness.

Acts 4:27-31

The Holy Spirit will always support each and every work that is initiated by God. But He won't support any work of the flesh. When we follow the Word of God and allow Him to have the lead, His power will be in us and surrounding us. As a result you will be able to speak the Word of God with boldness, without allowing the religious or political spirits to muzzle you. Especially in these days, the name of Jesus Christ is an offense to many people. In the Church you often see that people would rather talk about Jesus than with Him. And many Church members are way too busy to lay a set of rules upon people and to put a new yoke on the shoulders of (young) believers. And even in parts of the Church, terms such as "serve" and "humility" are considered to be dirty words. We must be very aware of what kind of teachings we allow in our minds and our hearts. We never test on the basis of opinions and/or rules of man or Churches. The only Truth is the Word of God, written in the Bible or spoken by the Holy Spirit. Anything that derives from that, no matter how holy or religious it sounds, is a lie. Remember, the people who had the biggest issue with Jesus were not the unbelievers but the believers. Not those who denied God, but who acknowledged Him. Those were the people who took offense to the teaching of Jesus. If He faced that kind of opposition from among the believers, then so will you. But greater is He Who is in you. With the power of the Holy Spirit in and around you, with the Anointing from the Anointed One, nothing and no one can stop you. But when you move and speak based on your own strength, knowledge, wisdom and understanding, you will fall and fail.

The life of Jesus was unique in every single way. So were all of His sayings. Some of the things He has said can easily be missed. But here is something remarkable. In His early ministry, Jesus said something special about the Anointing. Let's take a look at what He said first.

Moreover, when you fast, do not be like the hypocrites, with a sad countenance. For they disfigure their faces that they may appear to men to be fasting. Assuredly, I say to you, they have their reward. But you, when you fast, anoint your head and wash your face, so that you do not appear to men to be fasting, but to your Father who is in the secret place; and your

Father who sees in secret will reward you openly.
Matthew 6:17

This saying of Jesus doesn't stand on itself, but is part of three things that He mentioned. He said:

- When you do a charitable deed, do it in secret;
- When you pray, do it in the secret place;
- When you fast, do it secretly.

In all three cases, Jesus emphasized that you shouldn't do any of these things in the sight of man, for your own gain. So not to show people how good or religious you are. Instead, make no mention of it at all, but just do it in secret. All three sayings end with an awesome promise. In other words, if you follow these sayings of Jesus, then this is what happens:

…your Father who sees in secret will Himself reward you openly. (verse 4)
…your Father who sees in secret will reward you openly. (verse 6)
…your Father who sees in secret will reward you openly. (verse 18)

But if you don't follow these sayings of Jesus, then:

…you have no reward from your Father in heaven. (verse 1)
Assuredly, I say to you, they have their reward. (verse 5)
Assuredly, I say to you, they have their reward. (verse 16)

Jesus was teaching that any of these things is a matter between your heart and God's heart, not to be seen by man and not to gain for your own profit or honor. Not for any form of treasure on this earth. But when we zoom in to the last part of these three sayings, we see a couple of interesting facts appear. First of all, it shows that the personal use of Anointing Oil was a common thing among ordinary people. Secondly, and what almost always is missed, is the fact that Jesus was breaking a tradition here. It was not allowed to Anoint oneself during fasting and during the day of atonement, it was even strictly forbidden by rabbinical laws. An example of this can be seen when Daniel was fasting (Daniel 10:3). But the fact that Jesus was going directly against this rabbinical law was pretty remarkable, especially when you consider the reason why Jesus came to the earth and on what day the Anointing was forbidden.

By the lack of Anointing, people were able to see that you were fasting or mourning (2 Samuel 14:2). The lack of Anointing in the case of mourning was usually when someone passed away or when someone considered oneself under a curse. In both cases people who lacked the Anointing were supposedly in pain or sorrow. In the case of the Pharisees and Scribes, we know that many of them were just lacking the Anointing to show the people how religious they were. But in any other case, there was definitely something going on with people, when they lacked Anointing. And here is Jesus, telling the people to Anoint themselves, no matter what. That is remarkable. It went straight against all the religious rulings of the spirituals leaders. Especially when you consider the fact that the most important day to lack Anointing, was the day of atonement. By telling the people to Anoint themselves, no matter what, He fulfilled the prophecy from Isaiah 61, the same part that He used to reveal Himself as the Messiah. In that verse He mentioned His aim.

To comfort all who mourn, to console those who mourn in Zion, to give them beauty for ashes, the oil of joy for mourning, the garment of praise for the spirit of heaviness; that they may be called trees of righteousness, the planting of the Lord, that He may be glorified.
Isaiah 61:2-3

Our atonement has been made by Jesus Christ, the Son of the Living God. It is because of that reason that we never have to lack again, no matter in what area, but especially in the area of the Anointing. He paid for all of that. His sacrifice was thoroughly and more than sufficient. That's why Jesus told all the ordinary people never to stop Anoint themselves. Because there is no more reason for mourning. The price has been paid. Atonement has been made. It is finished. Sin has no more power over us, when we are in Jesus Christ. No more atonement is needed. Jesus Christ is sufficient. This so huge! So incredible! Jesus Christ became our Horn of Salvation (Luke 1:69), the Horn of David (Psalm 132:17), from Whom our spiritual Anointing flows.

An incredible example of someone who acted from the heart, instead of for the honor of man, was Mary. She wasn't out for her own gain. She wanted to give Jesus Christ the honor and the treatment that He deserved. What she did, she did from the heart. That is why it was an acceptable offer to Jesus. While the religious leaders refused to honor Him, by washing and Anointing Him, this 'sinful' woman came instead and gave Him the treatment that His host should have given Him. She gave all she could possibly give. For that reason she left with her sins forgiven and erased. For her gift came from the heart. That is all that matters to Jesus. He doesn't look down at the broken hearted, the wounded, at those who are in pain. He came to strengthen the weak, to comfort all who mourn, to give beauty for ashes, the oil of joy for mourning and the garment of praise for the spirit of heaviness. At that moment she didn't know that she did that for His burial. It was a Jewish custom to Anoint the dead, which is why Jesus said that she did it for His burial. By saying this, He announced His death. And although all the preparations were made to Anoint Him, after He died, He never was Anointed again on this earth. When they arrived at the tomb of Jesus, He was already risen (Mark 16:1-8). Therefore Mary was the last person who Anointed Him.

Assuredly, I say to you, wherever this gospel is preached in the whole world, what this woman has done will also be told as a memorial to her.
Matthew 26:13

Not only did Jesus become the Cornerstone, our Foundation, He also became the Capstone (Zachariah 4:7), which is the covering stone, holding our covering together. A capstone is the finishing stone of a structure. It is the stone that holds the roof together and it is also called the crowning achievement. He is the Alpha and the Omega, the Beginning and the End.

CHAPTER 14
THE BRIDE OF THE ANOINTED

When a time of mourning ended for someone, everyone was able to see that because of the resumption of the Anointing with Anointing Oil. It was the moment when the people allowed joy back in their lives. Occasions like these were also specifically mentioned during feasts, celebrations and victories. It is the image of rising above all the circumstances, of being lifted up. The image of overcoming.

Moreover those who were near to them, from as far away as Issachar and Zebulun and Naphtali, were bringing food on donkeys and camels, on mules and oxen—provisions of flour and cakes of figs and cakes of raisins, wine and oil and oxen and sheep abundantly, for there was joy in Israel.
1 Chronicles 12:40

You prepare a table before me in the presence of my enemies; You anoint my head with oil; my cup runs over.
Psalm 23:5

As Jesus so beautifully stated, our time of mourning has passed. The victory belongs to Jesus and to us, who are in Jesus. By accepting His name and His authority over you, by acknowledging Him as the Messiah and the Son of God, you became a part of something huge. The bride of Christ. The wonderful shining bride of Christ. As such, you are invited to the wedding of the Lamb. That wedding is about to happen soon. There is an event mentioned in the Scriptures, where Jesus promised that He will come to take His bride away from the earth and away from all the tribulations and destruction that are about to come over the earth. That event is called the rapture. It is probably the event that is discussed the most, heavily criticized, heavily questioned, laughed at and which is downsized and dismissed by many as a myth. But it will happen, whether people believe it or not. His Word is yes and amen. What Jesus has promised, will come to pass. We, the bride of Christ, are looking forward to that wonderful moment.

When we look at the situation in the world, we can all see that things are working towards the end, towards the closure of this era or eon. But although we know the present eon is coming to an end, nobody knows exactly when this eon will end and the next eon will begin. What we do know is that Jesus told us that He would come for us and that we need to be ready for it. That is at all times. We're not working towards a moment when we are ready. We need to be ready now. God's time is now. This hour, this minute, this second. For you don't know when He will come. But when He comes, you want to be ready.

Therefore you also be ready, for the Son of Man is coming at an hour you do not expect.
Matthew 24:44

Many Christians still live their lives as if the coming of the Lord is taking another dozens, hundreds or thousands of years. As if it will never happen in their lifetime. They live their lives as if there is always another tomorrow, always a change to get their life in order and to become the man or woman God wants them to be. His imminent coming is easily dismissed and compared with all the times when people expected Him and when He didn't come. They refer to all the false prophets, who predicted the day of the rapture, which came and passed. Therefore they are foolish enough to believe and assume that they are safe and that there is no need to be ready now. But the fact is that Jesus never gave any clues or any direction about the exact day of His coming, the day of the rapture. More than that, Jesus cannot give you those details, for He doesn't know. Jesus does not know on which day the rapture will take place. He does not know the time. So He can't tell us. Only His and our heavenly Father knows the day and the hour (Matthew 24:36, Mark 13:32). That means that no one can be sure, except the Father. It means that no one can assume that there will be another tomorrow, to get their lives in order and to be the person God wants them to be. So while Jesus couldn't tell us the day, He specifically told and instructed all of His followers to be ready at all times. To live our lives as if He can come at this moment, at this second.

"Then the kingdom of heaven shall be likened to ten virgins who took their

lamps and went out to meet the bridegroom. Now five of them were wise, and five were foolish. Those who were foolish took their lamps and took no oil with them, but the wise took oil in their vessels with their lamps. But while the bridegroom was delayed, they all slumbered and slept. "And at midnight a cry was heard: 'Behold, the bridegroom is coming; go out to meet him!' Then all those virgins arose and trimmed their lamps. And the foolish said to the wise, 'Give us some of your oil, for our lamps are going out.' But the wise answered, saying, 'No, lest there should not be enough for us and you; but go rather to those who sell, and buy for yourselves.' And while they went to buy, the bridegroom came, and those who were ready went in with him to the wedding; and the door was shut. "Afterward the other virgins came also, saying, 'Lord, Lord, open to us!' But he answered and said, 'Assuredly, I say to you, I do not know you.' "Watch therefore, for you know neither the day nor the hour in which the Son of Man is coming.
Matthew 25:1-13

Notice that all were slumbering and slept. Including the wise virgins. But the wise virgins slept assured, for they were ready. The foolish virgins slept in ignorance, not knowing what would happen and if they would have enough oil. But when the time came, all arose and only the wise had enough to enter the house with the bridegroom. They were prepared, because their love for the bridegroom resulted in actions, not just in empty words. They showed their love, what lived in their hearts, by their deeds. It was only at that moment that the foolish virgins realized that their oil was not sufficient. This is the difference between those who live by the Spirit and those who live by the law. Those who choose to be dependent and those who rather take matters into their own hands, using their own knowledge, wisdom and insight. These foolish virgins will miss the boat.

I am very aware of the numerous teachings and doctrines on the great tribulation and the rapture. There are many teachers, teaching that the bride of Christ has to go through the great tribulation. While I'm not willing to be a part of the many meaningless discussions on this area, nor do I want to take part in any debate on this matter, I will give you something to chew on, which is all I'm going to say about it.

But take heed to yourselves, lest your hearts be weighed down with carousing, drunkenness, and cares of this life, and that Day come on you unexpectedly. For it will come as a snare on all those who dwell on the face of the whole earth. Watch therefore, and pray always that you may be counted worthy to escape all these things that will come to pass, and to stand before the Son of Man.
Luke 21:34-36

If it would be true that the bride of Christ would have to go through the great tribulation, then what do we need to escape from? The thousands years of peace that follow? The moment of Armageddon, at the conclusion of those thousand years? None of both. This clearly talks about the coming destruction that will come over the earth, the great tribulation and the escape from it. For there are no worries in the thousand years of peace. The worries are in these days. They are everywhere around us. And they will increase greatly among the unbelievers. For the worries are designed by the enemy, in order to rob us of our focus on Jesus, and to put it on our circumstances. But the fact is that when all the events that Jesus described are beginning to happen, then our moment of escape is near. Therefore I want to advise you to study Luke 21, together with the Holy Spirit. The literal translation of Luke 21:36 says "Be vigilant in every season, on every occasion, and pray (constantly) that you may be deemed worthy to escape all these things that are about to happen and to stand in front of the Son of man."

In the book of Revelation, Jesus talks about the same moment, when He points out how we can become ready for the moment of the rapture. I also give you two other related Bible parts, to show you the bigger picture.

I counsel you to buy from Me gold refined in the fire, that you may be rich; and white garments, that you may be clothed, that the shame of your nakedness may not be revealed; and anoint your eyes with eye salve, that you may see.
Revelation 3:18

And I further answered and said to him, "What are these two olive

branches that drip into the receptacles of the two gold pipes from which the golden oil drains?
Zechariah 4:12

Let your garments always be white, and let your head lack no oil.
Ecclesiastes 9:8

There are two things that are needed in order to be ready for the rapture. The first is the gold of Jesus, the second is the white garments. The gold, that our heads and eyes are Anointed, the white garments, that we will not be naked and that our shame is covered. Both are available, but not for free. They are for sale. It will cost you. Otherwise it wouldn't be a purchase. Jesus offers it to us and He says that we need to buy it from Him. That has nothing to do with money. What He wants is your life. All of it. Including your heart, your thoughts, your decisions, your deeds, your body, your spirit, your soul, your house, your car, your job, everything. He wants to have a say about and over everything. He wants His Word to dwell in you. He wants His Words to become your words. His thoughts to become your thoughts. His sayings to become your sayings. His deeds to become your deeds. And in order to achieve that, you need total and utter dependency. And that is a choice you will have to make. It is also something we all need to learn, with the help of our Helper, the Holy Spirit. You need to come to the place where you realize that you can't do anything without Jesus. Not even changing yourself. We need to allow Him to do it in us. By keeping our focus on Him. By staying in His Word. By worshiping Him in spirit and in truth. By praying. By waiting. By persevering. By enduring.

The gold that Jesus is referring to is the heavenly Anointing. On several occasions the Bible calls the Anointing Oil "the gold", as can be seen in Zechariah 4:12. In this natural world, not all the olives can be used directly to make pure olive oil. There are several different olives, from different areas and different nations, with different tastes. They cannot all be blended together, for the different tastes and the dirty and oxidized olives will mess up the clarity and the pure taste of the good olives. So they are olives, they contain oil, but they cannot be used in their original condition. However, they can be used once they have all gone through a process of refining. This refining process involves fire. First, all the olives are crushed and pulverized, until all the oil which they contain has come out. The extracted oil is heated to extremely high temperatures. This allows the producers to also use the olives that are not in the best condition. Through the process of refining, the taste of all the oil is neutralized, the oil becomes clear and all of the oil becomes useable, as the liquid gold that the Bible talks about. So when Jesus talks about the gold, refined in the fire, He is talking about our lives being crushed and pulverized, until all our deepest intentions and motivations have been laid bare. The only way to get our true intentions and motivations out is through pain, through hardships and through trials. That is dying to self. Then all these intentions and motivations are being subjected to the test of His fire. All the impurities and bad tastes are removed and neutralized, until the only thing left is the pure refined gold.

The refined oil, the pure gold, becomes an excellent instrument in the hands of God. But through all of the pain, all of the hardships and all of the trials, He will never leave us alone. Not during the refining process and not during the moments we are allowed to minister in His service. He will be there every step of the way. Where every other friend will fail you and leave you, He will never walk away. Not even in your weakest moments. Jesus has promised us the Helper, our precious Holy Spirit, to stand by our side, to help us and to comfort us in times of need. To encourage us to go on, when we've come to the point we would rather give up. As mentioned before, the Anointing Oil is the image of the Holy Spirit. Do you remember the phrase "The oil of joy for mourning", from Isaiah 61:3? Did you know that one of the possible translations of this phrase can also be "The oil of rapture for mourning"? Now let's read this verse again with that translation.

"To console those who mourn in Zion, to give them beauty for ashes, the oil of rapture for mourning, the garment of praise for the spirit of heaviness; That they may be called trees of righteousness, the planting of the Lord, that He may be glorified."
Isaiah 61:1-3

In everything Jesus did and does, we can see His intentions to prepare us for the moment of the rapture and our wedding with Jesus Christ. The oil of rapture or the oil of joy is given to us for our preparation for the wedding. When a Jewish girl was getting married, it was accustomed that she brought in a portion or property into the marriage. This is also known as the dowry. In Israel, the bridegroom named a price or ransom to the father of the bride, which was called a mohar. That was the share the bridegroom had to bring in. However, it is not clear whether this mohar was given to the father of the bride or to the bride. In a spiritual sense, Jesus has named a price. His own life was the mohar, which He offered to the Father, as a ransom for us, His bride. Because of that, the heavenly Father became our Father as well. Now it is our heavenly Father who will offer a dowry to Jesus, in return for His ransom for us, to bring into our marriage with Jesus.

Now here's another beautiful part of that custom. The bride, on her turn, was and is allowed to ask for one tenth of the dowry, in the form of Anointing Oil, for her preparation for the wedding. When I discovered that old custom, I immediately realized that, in a spiritual sense, this is referring to the latter rain. We're talking about a heavy Anointing, not just another Anointing, but an Anointing that prepares us for our great moment at the wedding. But here's the thing. The bride didn't automatically receive one tenth of the dowry in the form of Anointing Oil. She would only receive it when she would ask for it. When I saw that, I immediately started to ask God if we, the bride of Christ, should ask for one tenth of our dowry. After all, I want to be ready for the marriage, and I believe that you feel the same way. So if there is a special dowry Anointing that we don't know of, I wanted to know about it, I wanted to know if that is the latter rain and if we should ask for it. The answer to that question came much faster than I expected. This was the response that the Holy Spirit gave me, in answer to those questions.

Ask the Lord for rain In the time of the latter rain. The Lord will make flashing clouds; He will give them showers of rain, grass in the field for everyone.
Zechariah 10:1

Wow, wow, wow! That is the dowry Anointing! So there will be a moment of heavy Anointing, a special dowry Anointing, the latter rain, in order to prepare us for the wedding. But we have to ask for it, in order to receive it. If we don't ask, we will not receive. Now what kind of Anointing is that latter rain exactly? Let's take a look in the book of Joel.

Be glad then, you children of Zion, And rejoice in the Lord your God; For He has given you the former rain faithfully, And He will cause the rain to come down for you— The former rain, and the latter rain in the first month.
Joel 2:23

Now this is, once again, extremely interesting, for I have read this passage before and studied its meaning. We know that God is a God of numbers and measures, even though we don't always know the exact numbers and measures He is using. But on several occasions in the Bible, you can see that God gives exact numbers and measures. Just like one tenth of our dowry is a measure as well, although we don't know how much that is exactly. But because of this verse from Joel, we can get some idea of what that must be like. This verse literally says that God gave the former rain "to just measure". Then it says that He will give the former rain, which refers to all the former revivals that have crossed the earth in the past, and which were apparently an exact just measure. And then He says that He will give the latter rain on top of that, all in the same season. Imagine! A revival Anointing plus a heavy revival Anointing. What does that equal? I have honestly no clue. But it must be huge. The testimonies of the past revivals already describe extreme heavy Anointings. Lives were being saved, healed, delivered and restored. At some times, the glory of God was so heavy that people weren't even able to walk. Then what can we expect when we receive that and when the latter rain is added to that? Although I cannot exactly answer that question, since nobody ever has witnessed that before on earth, I do know what the results will be. It will be the restoration of God's people on every possible level, including financially. It will be the outpouring of God's Spirit on all flesh. Signs, wonders and miracles will happen all over the earth. And all of this will happen before Jesus will come for His bride. When the measure of the former and the latter rain has been given, then this will happen.

The sun shall be turned into darkness, and the moon into blood, before the coming of the great and awesome day of the Lord. And it shall come to pass that whoever calls on the name of the Lord shall be saved.
Joel 2:31-32

There are exciting times ahead, but the outpouring of this Anointing doesn't automatically mean that people will respond properly. The Anointing will only cause change to those areas where you want to change. That means that our attitudes need to be aimed at the preparation of the wedding. It also means that we need to realize that the bride of Christ isn't you alone. It is you and all the children of God. It is you and all those whom God wants to save, heal, deliver and restore. We don't receive all of this for our own benefit. We receive in order to share. On every possible level. We need to realize that there is no "me" or "you" in the body of Christ, there is only "us". We are one, whether we like it or not. And it is for our own benefit that we're getting used to that, for it won't be any different in heaven and in eternity. And that brings us to the second part that Jesus talked about in Revelation 3:18. First He tells us to buy the gold, refined in fire. Then He says that we need garments. "White garments, that you may be clothed." Now what are these white garments? That is question is answered in the next verses.

Let us be glad and rejoice and give Him glory, for the marriage of the Lamb has come, and His wife has made herself ready." And to her it was granted to be arrayed in fine linen, clean and bright, for the fine linen is the righteous acts of the saints.
Revelation 19:7-8

Our wedding garments, the fine linen, are the righteous acts we have done. Not so long ago I saw a video teaching by Derek Prince, where I heard him say that the Church of today would probably have just enough material for a bikini. From what I have seen thus far, I must say that is correct. But Jesus says that our nakedness needs to be covered. How do we do that? By righteous acts. What is God's biggest concern? That there are people who will be lost. His biggest concern needs to be our biggest concern.

Woe to you who put far off the day of doom, who cause the seat of violence to come near; Who lie on beds of ivory, stretch out on your couches, eat lambs from the flock and calves from the midst of the stall; Who sing idly to the sound of stringed instruments, and invent for yourselves musical instruments like David; Who drink wine from bowls, and anoint yourselves with the best ointments, but are not grieved for the affliction of Joseph.
Amos 6:3-6

God is always going after the unsaved, in order to save them, He always stands up for the poor, the widows, the orphans and the oppressed, in order to care for them. He fights for them, like He fought for you. He cares for them, like He cares for you. He died for them, like He died for you. That is how much of a priority He gives to it. In the contemporary Church, salvation is a priority, but not the priority. Caring for the poor, the widows, the orphans, the oppressed... it is a priority, but a very low one. Why? Because we can do so much more. But that would actually cost us. It could mean that God asks us to give up a holiday and to use that money for one of His purposes instead. The restoration of finances and of everything else, will not automatically say that people will use the given resources in a good manner. People will still have a choice. What we usually see in the world is that the more money people get, the more afraid they are to lose it and the less they give. The Church is no different. It should be different, but it isn't. Yet. What we usually see in the world is that those who have very little, share all they can. And that attitude needs to remain the same when God restores everything in our lives. After all, we want more than just a bikini when we marry Jesus.

Watch therefore, for you do not know when the master of the house is coming—in the evening, at midnight, at the crowing of the rooster, or in the morning— lest, coming suddenly, he find you sleeping. And what I say to you, I say to all: Watch!
Mark 13:35-37

Are we courageous enough to buy the gold from Jesus? To clothe ourselves in the white garments? It starts with a choice from our end. We can simply ask God to make us ready, to prepare us, to do what He wants, when He wants it and how He wants it in our life. It will cost us a lot. It is the process where "I" is removed from the throne of our hearts and where Jesus takes His rightful highest place. That can be painful at the moment, but the gain will be so much more. At the moments of pain, trials and tribulations, it is hard to see what good can come from it. But when all of that is over, you can see and you will know why. And it will be more than worth it.

Therefore be patient, brethren, until the coming of the Lord. See how the farmer waits for the precious fruit of the earth, waiting patiently for it until it receives the early and latter rain. You also be patient. Establish your hearts, for the coming of the Lord is at hand.
James 5:7-8

In everything Jesus does for you, He prepares you for the wedding. The only thing we have to do is to follow His lead. Then we will become His Anointed Bride. Don't give up now. Your life means so much to Jesus. His love for you is so extremely great. He, Who sacrificed all for you, longs for you. I want to encourage you to not focus on your present situations and circumstances. These come, but they will just as surely go. Jesus is the only One Who comes and stays. Put your focus on Him and don't allow the enemy to rob you of it. And if you feel like you can take no more, then ask for the latter rain and hold fast. Help is on the way. The clouds are already gathering. Jesus will never give up on you.

Worship God! For the testimony of Jesus is the spirit of prophecy.
Revelation 19:10

Even so, come, Lord Jesus!
Revelation 22:20

ANOINTING IN THE BIBLE

OLD TESTAMENT

Genesis 8:11
Genesis 28:18
Genesis 31:13
Genesis 35:14
Exodus 23:11
Exodus 25:6
Exodus 27:20
Exodus 28:41
Exodus 29:2, 7, 21, 23, 29, 36, 40
Exodus 30:22, 24, 25, 26, 30, 31
Exodus 31:11
Exodus 35:8, 14, 15, 28
Exodus 37:29
Exodus 39:38
Exodus 40:9, 10, 11, 13, 15
Leviticus 2:1, 2, 4, 5, 6, 7, 15, 16
Leviticus 4:3, 5, 16
Leviticus 5:11
Leviticus 6:15, 20, 21, 22
Leviticus 7:10, 12, 36
Leviticus 8:2, 10, 11, 12, 26, 30
Leviticus 9:4
Leviticus 10:7
Leviticus 14:10, 12, 15, 16, 17
Leviticus 16:32
Leviticus 21:10, 12
Leviticus 24:2
Numbers 3:3
Numbers 4:9, 16
Numbers 5:15

Numbers 6:15
Numbers 7:1, 10, 13, 19, 25, 31, 37, 43, 49, 55, 61, 67, 73, 79, 84, 88
Numbers 8:8
Numbers 11:8
Numbers 15:4, 6, 9
Numbers 18:12
Numbers 28:5, 9, 12
Numbers 35:25
Deuteronomy 6:11
Deuteronomy 7:13
Deuteronomy 8:8
Deuteronomy 11:14
Deuteronomy 12:17
Deuteronomy 14:23
Deuteronomy 18:4
Deuteronomy 24:20
Deuteronomy 28:40, 51
Deuteronomy 32:13
Deuteronomy 33:24
Joshua 24:13
Judges 9:8, 9, 15
Judges 15:5
Ruth 3:3
1 Samuel 2:10, 35
1 Samuel 8:14
1 Samuel 9:16, 27
1 Samuel 10:1
1 Samuel 12:3, 5
1 Samuel 15:1, 17
1 Samuel 16:1, 3, 6, 12, 13
1 Samuel 24:6, 10
1 Samuel 26:9, 11, 16, 23
2 Samuel 1:14, 16, 21
2 Samuel 2:1, 4, 7
2 Samuel 3:39
2 Samuel 5:3, 17
2 Samuel 12:7, 20

2 Samuel 14:2
2 Samuel 15:30
2 Samuel 19:10, 21
2 Samuel 22:51
2 Samuel 23:1
1 Kings 1:34, 39, 45
1 Kings 5:1, 11
1 Kings 6:23, 31, 32, 33
1 Kings 17:12, 14, 16
1 Kings 19:15, 16
2 Kings 4:1, 2, 6, 7
2 Kings 5:26
2 Kings 9:1, 3, 6, 12
2 Kings 11:12
2 Kings 18:32
2 Kings 23:30
1 Chronicles 9:29
1 Chronicles 11:3
1 Chronicles 12:40
1 Chronicles 14:8
1 Chronicles 16:22
1 Chronicles 27:28
1 Chronicles 29:21, 22
2 Chronicles 2:10, 15
2 Chronicles 6:42
2 Chronicles 11:11
2 Chronicles 22:7
2 Chronicles 23:11
2 Chronicles 28:15
2 Chronicles 31:5
2 Chronicles 32:28
Ezra 3:7
Ezra 6:9
Ezra 7:22
Nehemiah 5:11
Nehemiah 8:15
Nehemiah 9:25

Jeremiah 40:10
Jeremiah 41:8
Lamentations 4:20
Ezekiel 16:9, 13, 18, 19
Ezekiel 23:41
Ezekiel 27:17
Ezekiel 28:14
Ezekiel 32:14
Ezekiel 45:14, 24, 25
Ezekiel 46:5, 7, 11, 14, 15
Daniel 9:24
Daniel 10:3
Hosea 2:5, 8, 22
Hosea 12:1
Hosea 14:6
Joel 1:10
Joel 2:19, 24
Amos 4:9
Amos 6:6
Micah 6:7, 15
Habakkuk 3:13, 17
Haggai 1:11
Haggai 2:12, 19
Zechariah 4:1, 3, 11, 12, 14
Zechariah 14:4

NEW TESTAMENT

Matthew 6:17
Matthew 21:1
Matthew 24:3
Matthew 25:3, 4, 8
Matthew 26:6, 7, 9, 12, 30
Mark 6:13
Mark 11:1
Mark 13:3
Mark 14:3, 4, 8, 26

Mark 16:1
Luke 4:18
Luke 7:37, 38, 46
Luke 10:34
Luke 16:6
Luke 19:29, 37
Luke 21:37
Luke 22:39
Luke 23:56
John 8:1
John 9:6, 11
John 11:2
John 12:1, 3, 5
Acts 1:12
Acts 4:27
Acts 10:38
Romans 11:17, 24
2 Corinthians 1:21
Hebrews 1:9
James 3:12
James 5:14
1 John 2:20, 27
Revelation 3:18
Revelation 6:6
Revelation 11:4
Revelation 18:13

ABOUT LOVEUNLIMITED

The biggest testimony in regard to Jesus Christ were not the signs and miracles. It were the lives that had been changed. And I'm talking about real change. The sort of change that friends, family and everyone you know would notice. It is the testimony "Jesus changed my life", while everyone is able to see and confirm it. God never changed. Jesus never changed. This still is the biggest testimony of all. It is huge. Change may not come in a day, but it will come as we keep our eyes fixed on Jesus. Real change. Hearts that are completely surrendered to Jesus. Lives that are completely restored. That is what LoveUnlimited is about.

Real change doesn't come from our own efforts. If we want the same results that Jesus had, we have to move and act in the same Spirit. Therefore we choose to be completely depended on the Holy Spirit, in everything we do. It is only the Word of God, through the power of Jesus Christ and by His Holy Spirit, that has the power to bring the real change. The sort of change that lasts. Our own efforts will just bring religion. The Holy Spirit will bring real change, and because of that there is freedom.

As darkness is increasing in the world like never before, we also see an increasing need among the people. Needs on all sorts of areas. To us that emphasizes how much we need God, especially in these days. As times are getting harder, naturally and spiritually, we see many people who fall back to old behaviors and some even turn their backs to Christianity. The main reasons for that are not understanding, pain, grief and disappointment.

We, as LoveUnlimited, want to reach out to the lost, the broken, the hurt, the poor, the rejected and to those where everyone looks down on. Our heart goes out to the people who are considered as unimportant and unworthy by most of the Church and by society. Not just in a faraway country, but starting in our nation, in our own cities and in our own neighborhoods. For if it doesn't start there, it has no value. If we only want to help those who are far away, we're just keeping up appearances. Real change shows fruits. Real change wants to help the needy, regardless of their needs. Real change creates an environment of grace, with room for error. Real change stands with people, not above them. We turn the real change in action so that:

People can be reached with the message of the cross and salvation
People can experience the power of real change, through Jesus Christ
All the unloved can experience the love of Father God
All the rejected can experience the acceptance of Father God
All the broken can experience the restoration that Jesus Christ has made available
All the hurt can experience the comfort of the Holy Spirit
All spiritual wounded people can find a place where they receive care
All those who want to grow to spiritual maturity can find a place to actually grow
(New) believers can be equipped to become disciples of Jesus Christ
We do so by:

Testifying about and leading people to Jesus Christ
Praying for the baptism in Spirit and in fire
Teaching people to become depended on the Holy Spirit
Just being there for people and by taking the time to listen
Not standing above people, but with them
In order to reach people and to be available, we organize theme-evenings, seminars and conferences. But we also offer free teachings on our websites and our YouTube Channel. Our websites offer the possibility for people to send their prayer requests as well. This is the work we have done unofficially since 2003 and officially since 2006. For as long as the Lord allows us, we will continue to do so.

Made in the USA
Middletown, DE
28 January 2018